The Progressed Moon Around the Zodiac

Charting Personal Development with Astrology

Gisele Terry, M.A.

Copyright 2011 by Gisele Terry

No part of this book may be reproduced or transcribed in any form or by any means, electronic or mechanical, including photocopying or recording or by any information storage and retrieval system without written permission from the author and publisher, except in the case of brief quotations embodied in critical reviews and articles. Requests and inquiries may be mailed to: American Federation of Astrologers, Inc., 6535 S. Rural Road, Tempe, AZ 85283.

ISBN-10: 0-86690-617-7
ISBN-13: 978-0-86690-617-3

Cover Design: Jack Cipolla

Published by:
American Federation of Astrologers, Inc.
6535 S. Rural Road
Tempe, AZ 85283

www.astrologers.com

Printed in the United States of America

Contents

Introduction	v
Chapter 1, Astrology: A Developmental Discipline?	1
Chapter 2, Converging Models: Astrology and Development Psychology	7
Chapter 3, The Moon and Dyadic Processes of Growth	17
Chapter 4, Theoretical Foundations for the Lunar Return Model of Development	27
Chapter 5, The Lunar Return Model of Development: Span of Attachment	33
Chapter 6, The Lunar Return Model of Development: Span of Relationship and Span of the World	41
Chapter 7, The Zodiac: Developmental Themes for Life	47
Chapter 8, Rotations and Revelations of the Secondary Progressed Moon	53
Chapter 9, Repetitive Themes on the Circular Pathway of Development	77
Chapter 10, Order and Chaos: Universal Patterns of Development	97
Endnotes	107
References	115

Introduction

Both psychology and astrology have developmental theories that explain how people grow from infancy through adulthood. As a psychotherapist and astrologer I work with these theories because they offer ways to understand clients' problems. The purpose of this book is to establish a model of astrological development called the lunar return model of development. It is based upon a merger of the two disciplines, psychology and astrology, and it focuses on the natal Moon, the progressed Moon, and the cycles of the progressed Moon around the zodiac.

It was several years after I started giving astrological consultations that I began to notice the significance of the progressed Moon. I began to see the progressed Moon as an indicator of a client's here and now emotional focus. The position of the progressed Moon, its sign and placement in the chart, became a starting point for my readings and provided additional access to the meaning of charts. In time a hypothesis about development in astrology emerged from my observations.

There is a correlation between the procession of signs in the zodiac and stages of development in psychology. The signs represent developmental stages because their meanings are comparable to the earliest phases of life in which formative emotional attachments are made or broken and set the stage for everything in life that follows. Psychology can offer astrology the most current understanding of human development, and of its application to chart interpretation. Astrology can offer psychology a unique view of the trajectory of development. Astrology demonstrates that development is not just linear, as it is in traditional psychology, but cyclical through the progressed Moon's motion around the zodiac. And as the progressed Moon travels through the signs around the chart, not just once or twice, but sometimes up to three times in a lifespan, it resonates with its own past as it cycles. Themes of life in one cycle around the horoscope can be revisited in the next. In each successive cycle it is possible to find opportunities to achieve more mature, adaptive modes of responding to critical life issues.

Chaos, or complexity, theory describes how systems that are not consistently stable—from water and cloud formations, to families, to economic and sociological trends—exchange energy with their environments, become more complex as they change over time, and yet maintain their structural integrity[1]. The astrology chart itself, particularly through the movement of the progressed Moon, can be understood in terms of these non-linear dynamic processes that occur in nature. The Moon continuously triggers patterns in the natal or progressed chart by sign, by house, or by aspect. It catalyzes dynamics in the form of aspects and aspect patterns similar to the processes that supply external information to a system, and thereby trigger energy exchanges between all points in the system as it moves towards higher levels of complexity. The horoscope, which is the system, and the Moon, which generates emergent processes, co-evolve patterns of development that are both constant and ever changing at the same time.

This book is divided into three sections. The first explains how ideas about development in astrology have corresponded with psychological theories of development. This analysis is the foundation for the hypothesis about an astrological model of growth based upon the progressed Moon, called the lunar return model of development. The second section describes this model in detail and uses case examples to illustrate how development through cycles of the progressed Moon shapes people's lives. And the third section illustrates the application of this lunar return model of development in clients' natal and progressed charts. This section also presents the possibility of the existence of a universal template for human development.

In order to arrive at this hypothesis about development in astrology, I have used an interdisciplinary approach. I have attempted to establish a unity of information by merging different bodies of knowledge. I have attempted to bring developmental psychology and astrology together to create a coherent understanding about human growth that would not have been evident by studying just one of these disciplines alone.

This model of development integrates other bodies of knowledge in addition to astrology and developmental psychology. I have drawn on systems theory, Rupert Sheldrake's bio-morphic field theory, neuroscience, and chaos theory, to make correlations intended to illuminate and substantiate my ideas. As with all theories, the ideas presented here may not apply for everyone, in all situations. It is open ended. It asks questions rather than assuming answers.

This work is based upon the tropical zodiac and the secondary progressed Moon. Although the Moon in all kinds of astrology is very important, it would not convey the same meaning in developmental terms that I am proposing here. The reason for this is that in the secondary progressions the Moon moves quickly, traveling through each of the twelve signs of the zodiac every two years and three or four months. It is because of this that there is a correspondence between the signs of the zodiac in astrology and the process of growth in developmental psychology in the cycle of a lunar return.

In bridging the worlds of astrology and developmental psychology, I am expressing a specific view. This relates to astrology's position and how it references itself in the world. Astrology has found inspired niches in intellectual studies of different origins. It finds itself reflected in lineages of its own tradition and in exciting discoveries of methodologies that provide new applications of astrology. Mythology and fairy tales have enhanced the interpretation of astrological symbols. Jungian psychology and analytical psychology provide familiar templates that mirror the symbolic language of the astrology chart. The world-view of archetypes—the mother, father, shadow, anima, and animus—is reflected in the meanings of symbols in the astrology chart. Other psychological theories—object relations theory, systems theory and narrative theory—have all been creatively and intuitively applied to astrological assessments and interpretations.

But astrology's frame of reference can expand even further. We need to speak in many languages in order to understand the breadth and width of symbols that embrace all recorded time—from the concepts born in past history to concepts that have just been formulated within the first years of the twenty-first century. The language of astrological symbols is enriched when its living tradition is infused with new paradigms. The hybrid of ideas that emerges when two apparently unrelated subjects are blended together is called "consilience." Here astrology is combined with the more traditional and mainline study of developmental psychology to yield something more than the sum of the two.

Knowledge of human development is an essential study for astrologers. Astrology itself is designed for this study. For many years astrologers have used developmental psychology in chart interpretation. However, understanding the most current ideas about how individuals mature can give astrologers an additional level of awareness to integrate into their work with clients. Astrologers who desire an understanding of human growth can benefit by knowing how human development is defined by recent research in neuroscience and developmental psychology.

The same principles that govern many non-linear complex systems of life govern astrology. Living systems, such as the organization of the brain in neuroscience, molecular structures in biology, evolution of human beings, family systems, and societies all operate according to the same principles that organize the astrology chart. We live in a world linked together in multiple systems of structures that reflect over and over again a universal developmental pattern. In astrology the progressed Moon conveys that this pattern is both psychological and metaphysical. Whether it renders a subtle or unconscious effect, or an overt and conscious one, the progressed Moon demonstrates that development unfolds uniquely for each person in accordance with this universal design as it passes through the signs of the zodiac and around the astrology chart.

Chapter One

Astrology: A Developmental Discipline

The purpose of this book is to present the lunar return model of development and to show how the newest concepts about human development can be integrated in the symbol of the Moon and the Moon's progressed cycles.

The lunar return model of development describes a process of human growth from infancy through the lifespan. This model illustrates how the signs of the zodiac correlate with stages of development from birth to twenty-seven and a third years, which is the exact amount of time it takes the secondary progressed Moon to make its lunar return—that is to travel from the moment of birth around the astrology chart and back to its natal position. The secondary progressed Moon symbolizes developmental themes as it passes through the signs of the zodiac and around the chart, not just once but up to three times in a life span. The same challenges that emerge during the first twenty-seven and a third years, repeat in the second, and even third cycles of the same length, but at levels of more life experience and chronological growth. Because of this, the repetition of themes in successive cycles can create opportunities to revisit and repair the past. Revisit and do it all over again but differently.

Before explaining how the lunar return model of development makes use of the latest discoveries in human development, it is important to acknowledge that the longstanding models of human growth, both in developmental psychology and astrology, still have credibility and applicability. In psychology these models originated over a century ago and describe fundamental aspects of psychological growth—emotional, sexual, cognitive, moral, and linguistic. They span a continuum from biological theories of maturation on one end to social learning theories of development on the other, with models that blend the two, as well[1]. In astrology there have been meaningful maps of development in both western and eastern traditions. In western astrology this map is an 84-year life cycle, the time it takes the planet Uranus to complete its full return to the position it occupied at a person's birth. Within this time cycles of all other planets and nodes represent maturation in many areas of human growth. In Indian astrology, the Dasha system offers an understanding of life process in a sequence of nine developmental periods, each with its own planetary ruler. The entire time for all nine Dashas to complete their assigned duration is 120 years because it is estimated that an average person of sound health, physically and spiritually, should live that long[2].

If there have been useful models of human growth in astrology, why should astrologers be interested in the subject of developmental psychology as it is conceptualized by psychologists and scientists? Furthermore, even if the subject of developmental psychology can have relevance to the work of astrology, how would it even be incorporated into the body of knowledge of development that already exists in astrology?

The answer is, in my opinion, that developmental psychology offers additional meanings to astrological symbols that would not otherwise be evident. Developmental psychology has already been integrated by many counseling astrologers who work in a psychological orientation. Information from recent discoveries in developmental psychology can also be easily assimilated into the signs of the zodiac and the symbol of the Moon.

The work of astrologers has always concerned the evolution of human life in accordance with planetary phases and cycles. In this specific regard, astrologers have an awareness that is similar to developmental psychologists. True, astrologers who counsel clients are not psychologists in an academic and scientific sense. They are counselors of a unique nature because they can utilize the language of cycles and symbols to describe individual growth, a language foreign to the work of traditional psychology. And this language of cycles and symbols translates into a developmental form that has multiple levels of meaning that are different from linear development in psychology.

Imbued in every aspect of our work are descriptions of cycles of growth that occur through planetary movements. We equate these cycles of growth with specific internal challenges and achievements—with emotional maturity (lunar return), with the coming into adulthood (Saturn return), with expansion of self (Jupiter), with the individuation process (Uranus); and for every planet and the nodal cycle we envision a process of development and growth. An interpretation of an astrology chart addresses an individual's life from the perspective of these cycles. This is a developmental perspective.

Astrologers pursue a quest of knowledge of the heavens in order to understand its impact on human lives. We want to know what planetary influences change people's lives—externally and internally—in order to help them. And based upon an understanding of human existence, astrologers draw connections and interpretations between the symbolic language of astrology and life experience. These interpretations, based on cycles of the planets, are developmental.

Astrology describes human evolvement within stages of luminary, planetary, and nodal cycles. And these descriptions are generally formulated in terms of humanistic philosophy. For astrologers, humanistic philosophy has contributed the most important basis for interpreting cycles of human growth in the twentieth century. The humanistic philosophy that appears in astrology originates in the humanistic movement which had a great influence on all the social sciences of the twentieth century.

The humanist movement emerged in the 1960s. It has a tradition of many roots going back centuries throughout many parts of the world. In fact, humanistic beliefs have been expressed throughout history any time human dignity and freedom of expression has been repressed.[3] It was reborn in the 1960s as a psychological movement, and its proponents envisioned human development in terms of organic and humanistic principles. Humanistic psychology of the 1960s was a reactionary movement—a reaction against the notion of the human psyche being dark and flawed, limited by conditions of early childhood as psychoanalysis had been contending. It reacted against the malevolent social forces of World War I and World War II by presenting hope for the spirit of human nature.

Humanism states that as long as development is neither interrupted nor required to conform to external standards of achievement, it moves organically in the direction of growth and self-discovery. Humanism promotes man's quest for self-actualization[4], a state of understanding one's true purpose in life. The humanistic philosophy affirms that the natural tendency of human nature is toward goodness and wholeness and the natural tendency of man is to develop in the direction of purpose and self-realization.

Astrologers became connected with humanistic philosophy in the 1960s.[5] We were incorporated into its field through the work of many prominent thinkers whose work influenced each other, such as psychologists Abraham Maslow and Carl Rogers, astrologers Dane Rudyhar and Alexander Ruperti, and Carl Jung as both psychologist and astrologer. Because humanistic philosophy is a tradition that views human growth in the context of its greater meaning and purpose, it is a perfect fit for the work of astrologers. Carl Rogers (1902-1987) proposed that the individual's natural motivation to learn and grow needs to be encouraged through confronting problems and attempting to master them. Through this struggle, new skills, capacities, and views about life are formed. Rogers called this a "person" or "client-centered" approach to therapy.[6]

There are four essential principles for the humanist movement:
1. The subjective experience of a person is more important than observational facts.
2. Human choice, creativity, and self-actualization, are the goals to be cultivated.
3. Meaningfulness is more important than objectivity.
4. Human dignity is the ultimate value.

Carl Jung (1875-1961) saw the unconscious as driven by the process of individuation, a drive toward wholeness and balance between the contradicting forces of the psyche. Like Rogers and Maslow, Jung felt that the unconscious is a source of health and vitality. He brought this same philosophy to his study of astrology[7], viewing the inherent tendency of the psyche to evolve toward integration and individuation, especially in the second part of life.

As astrologers, we give expression to the humanistic philosophy when we speak with clients about realizing the meaning of their lives through the challenges of patterns in their charts.

When we promote these patterns holistically without assigning aspects or transits, the stigma of "good" or "bad," we are thinking as humanists.

When we encourage clients to use difficult energies to grow and heal, we communicate as humanists.

Whenever we endorse the idea that our charts do not imprison us and astrological configurations are not restricted to one meaning only, we are thinking as humanists.

When we are optimistic for clients—holding out the possibility that they will experience patterns and cycles in their charts as prompts to personal growth and their unique life story—we are thinking as humanists. In astrology as well as psychology the essence of the humanistic spirit is the development of one's true inner self.

The idea that an astrology chart represents potential for psycho-spiritual development arose out of the movement in astrology that Dane Rudhyar pioneered in the 1960s. Prior to his work in humanistic astrology there was no theory about how the astrology chart conveys an individual's highest potential or about the path towards self-realization in a holistic sense. In general, astrologers were likely to put emphasis on character analysis, on whether positions were good or bad indications for future concerns, or upon events portended by astrological positions. More often there was a notion of phases and cycles that were fated, event-oriented (outer-oriented) and directive. Predictions carried the foreboding of good and bad outcomes. Interpretation was oriented toward descriptions of personality qualities that invited inevitable events.

Dane Rudhyar (1895-1985) changed all of this. A supporter of Carl Rogers, he called his astrology "person-centered astrology"[8] as a way to identify its humanistic philosophy and practice. Dane Rudhyar's lunation cycle contains a developmental theme that extends beyond one lifetime. In his model, having been born into one lunation phase, the soul returns in each lifetime to be born into the next for a total of eight lunation phases, and then goes around again. Rudhyar reformulated the perception of moments of time in astrology. He took the traditional view of planets out of the context of discreet moments and isolated states. He realized that any two planets exist in relationship to each other in the context of a continuum of movement around the zodiac.

The birth chart captures just one moment in time (one relational phase) of these two planets on this moving cycle. Every angular relationship that the faster moving planet makes after birth to the other planet by progression or transit is an expression of the ongoing phases of their dyadic development. These planets will fulfill every angular relationship possible in a person's lifetime in order to express their intention. Their conjunction is the seed moment, their opposition a culmination of tension between them, and their return to conjunct one another is their resolution.

The lunation cycle is used extensively to understand the relationship between the Sun and the Moon's phases, and their relationship to each other, both natal and progressed, as they travel around the zodiac. In addition, Dane Rudhyar introduced an approach to working with astrology in a psycho-spiritual context, to help the client become aware that the purpose of astrology is for human growth and not for predicting events good or bad that will befall the client. According to Rudhyar the chart holds the key to understanding how every person's life can proceed to its highest purpose, utilizing both the inherent gifts and challenges of astrological cycles.

Another contributor to humanistic astrology was Alexander Ruperti. He illustrated how planetary cycles and returns intersect with each other as they ascend the stages of life: "Astrology as the study of cycles becomes a study of the pattern or plan of what Jung called the individuation process , revealing in symbolic language how each person can fully become what he potentially is."[9] The planetary cycles relate to areas of development that are common for all people. They coincide and overlap with each other, creating a rich tapestry of meaning. Ruperti brought synthesis to the understanding of astrological cycles, particularly to the order of their critical years in an individual's life as well as their interconnections and intersections as phases of development.

Bruno and Louise Huber also conveyed a humanistic view of astrology in *Astrololgical Psychosynthesis*[10]. Their article, "Age Progressions," offers another astrological model of development across the entire lifespan.

For all these astrologers—Rudhyar, Ruperti, and the Hubers—the purpose of a life, the capacity for self-actualization, is reflected in the pattern of the birth chart. There is no "bad" aspect or transit, only ones that exist to challenge development and further its course. Not everyone realizes his or her full life potential and therefore one of the goals of humanistic astrology is to help people do just that—use conscious awareness of the astrology chart to fulfill their maximum potential. Patterns at birth, by progression, or by transit pose energetic and psychological trials en route to realizing one's self. Progressions represent the changing energetic and psychological dynamics that are measured in symbolic time (a day for a year, a month for a year, etc.) and can direct the movement of life toward its internal fulfillment. Transit cycles occur in many time frames (daily, monthly, yearly, etc.) and exert pressures upon the developing psyche to confront and adapt to external circumstances, thereby reorganizing internal life. Progressions and transits are co-determinants of the path of self-realization.

So astrologers are already developmental psychologists of a metaphysical kind who have taken a humanistic view to human growth. This humanistic view is a philosophy about respect for the intrinsic growth process of every human being. It places high regard for everyone's unique path to finding purpose and meaning in life. The humanistic view of development has been a perfect fit for astrology. Person centered, it offers the astrologer an approach to chart interpretation that prioritizes the internal experience of the client as part of a holistic developmental path towards self-realization and growth. It brings an internal focus to the practice of working with prediction. It reframes deterministic outcomes of patterns and cycles with interpretations that concern the growth of the inner psyche. Humanistic astrology transformed the practice of astrology, once governed by absolutism and literal prediction, to a practice of possibility, hope, and meaning.

Chapter Two

Converging Models: Astrology and Developmental Psychology

Knowledge about human development has been the quest of many sciences and traditions, not just developmental psychology and astrology. Chemistry, biology, neuroanatomy, neurology, ethology, linguistics, and anthropology are some of the disciplines that have provided sources of the information we have to date about human evolution.

Recently the field of developmental psychology has been greatly influenced by discoveries in the fields of neuroscience and genetics. Developmental psychology is the study of how infants and children mature in several categories of growth. There are theories of emotional development, moral development, language development, learning development, and social development. For more than a century the models that have shaped our understanding of these areas of development have generally been divided into two groups: stage theories and learning theories. Stage theories maintain that internal and intrinsic forces guide human development. Learning theories propose that culture and the external environment structure development by modeling, teaching, rewarding or conditioning human behavior. Examples of this are Montessori's learning theory, Bandura's social modeling theory, and Skinner's theory of conditioned responses.[1]

Stage (bio-genetic) theories and learning (environmental) theories represent deeply divergent views of growth. Yet in application, models blend or blur their distinctions. From the 1940s to present, most psychological theories use a combination of stage and learning theories to explain the origins of mental and emotional disorders. Working with children and adults in psychotherapy necessitates a creative understanding of how many developmental models intersect and describe the unique developmental process of every individual.

All models—biological and environmental—have critical periods when growth either springs from a preset timing or has windows of opportunity through social and environmental conditioning. In all theories, growth is hierarchical, one level assimilated by the next at successively more complex levels.[2]

Stage theories provide a useful form for comparing development models in psychology with those in astrology. The predominant features of stage theories are: 1) development unfolds in biologically preset and unvarying sequences, 2) from one stage to the next, growth is qualitatively different, resulting in entirely new structures, 3) each stage has general attributes and behaviors that can be applied across a wide variety of tasks, 4) each stage is its own whole unit, with characteristics not less than the next, and 5) development follows the same sequences in all cultures; different cultures may teach different beliefs and have different emotional values that influence the expression of development, but the underlying structural stages of development are biologically preprogrammed on a universal scale.

Some stage theories are purely maturational, meaning that sequences are age specific, and biologically pre-set to emerge at certain times in life. Crawling occurs for infants at about nine months and walking at about twelve months[3]. In other stage theories the rate of growth may vary but the sequencing remains the same. For example, moral development that is based upon internal convictions of right and wrong always follows moral development that is based upon reward and punishment, but the exact age of advancement to more mature moral judgment may be different from one person to the next.

Some stage models of development, like Piaget's cognitive development and Kohlberg's moral development[4], do not originate entirely in genetic pre-programming. They are part genetic in origin and part intrinsic, arising out of spontaneous curiosity and interest, not out of predetermined phases. While neither Piaget nor Kohlberg would refute the influence of genetics on cognitive and moral growth, the primary belief is that there is a unique way each child arrives at this. Yet intrinsic growth seems to arrange itself in stages, each one organizing constructs of multiple abilities at more complex levels. Some children remain longer in one stage than another, and some children never graduate to the more complex cognitive and moral levels of development. What makes the difference depends upon each child's nature and environmental conditioning.

Psychoanalysis has always utilized stage theories for the treatment of mental and emotional disorders in children and adults. Psychoanalytic stage theories have a combination of the features of maturational and intrinsic models of development. The particular province of development in psychoanalytic stage theories, however, is the inner world of feeling, fantasy, dreams, impulses and the unconscious mind.

In the earliest stage models, from the early 1900s to mid-century, growth in its purest sense is internal, not affected by the external environment or relationship with primary caregivers. In these models, the mother for the most part need only be physically present because development unfolds on its own.

Gradually theories of development arose that recognized how the actual relationship between infant and mother and infant and other primary relationships shape internal psychic structures. Then, during the 1950s, stage theories became a conceptual mix of biologically predetermined growth and the effects of early relationships and environment.

Up until the 1950s, mental and emotional disorders in adults who sought psychoanalysis were seen as derivatives of problems in early developmental stages—problems that were either never fully mastered or never integrated.

Psychoanalysis focused on what went wrong in emotional development and, furthermore, the nature of emotional development was deduced, not observed. Whatever constitutes "normal infant to adult development" was not a subject of analysis[5]. Only in the late 1950s to 1960s was normal development chronicled from observing children in real time relationships with their mothers. This normal development has also been formulated in stage theories.

Many traditions, both scientific and metaphysical, have utilized the design of the stage theory to understand human development, and astrology is among them. Astrology's stage theory is structured by the helix of planets and the Lunar Nodes, intertwined in cycles of different durations. Human growth represented through astrology follows a pre-set and hierarchical order, as do stage theories in developmental psychology. This is true in both western and eastern astrology.

In Indian astrology, the Dasha system offers an understanding of the process of life in a sequence of nine developmental periods, each with its own planetary ruler. The entire time for all nine Dashas to complete their assigned duration is 120 years because it is estimated that an average person of sound health, physically and spiritually, should live that long. In western astrology, phases of planetary cycles (i.e., first Saturn square, Saturn opposition, second Saturn square, Saturn return) are very much like stages in maturational theories of traditional psychology. The full life cycle is eighty-four years, the time it takes for a complete Uranus return. Within these eighty-four years the cycles of the Moon, Jupiter, Saturn, Uranus and the Moon's Nodes interconnect at prescribed times.

The full potential of an astrology chart unfolds as progressions and transits traverse over angles and planets in the chart at timed intervals. Some cycles complete and repeat more than once in a lifetime, creating second or third returns. Parts of cycles—one half cycle, one third of a complete cycle, or one sixth of a complete cycle, like transiting Uranus sextile natal Uranus—convey that repetition of an experience has a unique place in the process of growth.

Another similarity between developmental psychology and astrology is that stages of human growth in psychology coincide with these planetary cycles. Stages in both disciplines represent milestones associated with specific challenges and achievements. In addition, the structures of development, the sequencing of growth stages in both science and astrology, are pre-set and deterministic and proceed in prescribed periods of time.

The stages of cycles in astrology are universal just like the milestones in theories of developmental psychology. They happen for everyone in the same sequence. In science this is supported by research in cross-cultural developmental psychology. In astrology this pre-set order occurs in the timing of planetary cycles in accordance with both the physical and metaphysical laws of nature.

The lunar return model of development introduces new concepts about the correlations between astrology and developmental psychology through the signs and configuration of the Moon, the fact is that the correspondence between the two disciplines already exists in the body of astrological knowledge. The associations between planetary cycles and well-researched transitions of growth have been in the awareness of those counseling astrologers who work with developmental themes. And traditional interpretations in astrology about these cycles of development that correspond to planetary cycles are as valid today as they were a decade or two ago.

For example, Mars returns, Jupiter returns, and Saturn returns all coincide with known stages of development in psychology and continue to be very useful tools for the astrologer who interprets developmental cycles. Astrologers who work on children's charts refer to the first Mars return because it coincides with the "terrible two's." The first quarter Saturn return (seven years), the first opposition (fourteen years), the third quarter (twenty-one years), and full Saturn return at twenty-nine and a half years correspond to periods marked by increased awareness of reality, responsibility, and movement into adulthood. Interwoven with the Saturn cycle is the Jupiter cycle. Alexander Ruperti[6] advocates observing the cycles of

Jupiter and Saturn together, as their influences interrelate with periods of growth and expansion, and acceptance of limits and challenges of responsibility. At three, six, and nine years of age, Jupiter's influence is evident in a child's need for exploration, expansion, and rebellion. The first full Jupiter return occurs at age twelve. The same occurs again at ages fifteen, eighteen, and twenty-one. Jupiter's influence is felt again, every three years until age twenty-four when another full Jupiter return is complete[7]. All these are ages in which leaps of physical, cognitive and social growth occur, verified through research in developmental psychology. The cycle of Uranus also correlates with periods of development. It makes a semi-sextile to its birth position at age six and then a trine to its natal position at ages thirteen and twenty-eight, all ages of exploration and assertion of individuality.

Specific theories of development in psychology support meanings acribed to planetary cycles in astrology. These include the theories of Jean Piaget (cognitive development), Laurence Kohlberg (moral development), Margaret Mahler (emotional development),[8] Erik Erikson (development over the lifespan)[9], and the work of political and social journalist Gail Sheehy[10]. The following is a chart of age progression and the planet that rules the development that generally takes shape from infancy through the first Saturn return.

Age	Planet	Description
Age 2	Mars	Anger and oppositional behavior express separation
Age 3	Jupiter	Exploring the world through separation process
Age 6	Jupiter	Expansion of vocabulary and imaginative play
Age 7	Saturn	Age of reason and awareness of reality
Age 9	Jupiter	Increase in cognitive abilities, math, and science
Age 12	Jupiter	Expansion of social awareness and skills
Age 13	Uranus	First onset of puberty and rebellion/individuation
Age 14	Saturn	Advancement in social and moral responsibility
Age 15	Jupiter	Greater intimacy in relationships with both genders
Age 18	Jupiter	Need for freedom and advanced education
Age 21	Saturn/Jupiter	Freedom, with new responsibilities
Age 24	Jupiter	Greater social networks and community
Age 27⅓	Moon	Full emotional growth cycle
Age 28	Uranus	New awareness of individuality
Age 29½	Saturn	Sense of maturity and self-discipline

At age two, the first Mars return correlates with everything observed in toddlers. Development of control over motor skills is one of the goals of this age (one to three).

Anger, oppositional behavior, and "no" saying, are ways the toddler begins to separate from mother and father, a natural and necessary step in psychological growth. Egocentrism[11] is the thinking modality of toddlers, the "me,""mine," and "I want," and the need for immediate gratification. In Erikson's lifespan model, age two is the Autonomy vs. Shame stage and, in Mahler's model, it is the Rapprochment stage. Both refer to the toddler's internal conflict. One part of this conflict expresses assertion of will, of holding on to what he wants, and pushing away want he does not want. But this desire to establish autonomy is in conflict with the desire to cling to parents for emotional security. When the need for autonomy prevails, the word no or anger is expressed.

The first Jupiter trine to its own natal position occurs at ages three to four. This correlates with the need to explore, to use play as a vehicle of exploring reality, and to challenge oneself physically. Erikson's second stage in his eight stages of man is the initiative vs. guilt phase that dominates the three to four age range. The child makes plans and perseveres in trying to attain them, but then must accept that there are limits to what can be accomplished. By ages three to four in Mahler's separation individuation model, the child can attain full "object constancy" and can explore the world without the anxiety of earlier years because now he can retain an image of mother in his mind. Social development occurs at this age, often modeled as pro-social behaviors of sharing and reciprocity. These pro-social behaviors will develop into more friendship and social skills by age six. And even though ages three and four are still ages when thinking is egocentric, there is a greater awareness of other people.

Between the ages of six and eleven, awareness of reality in general increases as involvement in fantasy life decreases. In Erikson's model it is the third period, the Industry vs. Inferiority stage that is prominent now. Astrologically, Jupiter and Saturn cycles are strong at this juncture in development and represent both the external social development that can be attained as well as the internal awakening of a sense of one's limits. The grandiosity of earlier years yields to acceptance of real abilities and of the practice necessary to build skills. Children at this age are governed more by internal moral standards than just external rules. The goal here is mastery of real life skills and developing different competencies. But this is also a time when there can be a propensity for feeling inferior or inadequate. In Piaget's cognitive development model and Kohlberg's moral development model, ages six through eleven are a time when rules are thought of as fixed and immutable, and moral judgments are made on the basis of consequences. All kinds of development are processing and the correlations are easily drawn with both Jupiter and Saturn.

Jupiter makes its first full return at age twelve, a time of further cognitive and moral development. Thinking becomes more sophisticated, and there is the ability to make cause-

and-effect analyses. Based upon Kohlberg's theory of moral development, moral judgment is now more sophisticated because it is based on internal standards rather than consequences of actions. Social behavior is more sophisticated and the need to belong to a peer group becomes especially important. Because pro-social learning was modeled and practiced in early social relationships, the child can now establish himself in a world of more sophisticated peer relationships.

As Uranus makes its first sextile to itself at age thirteen, it mirrors Erikson's phase of identity vs. confusion in the lifespan model. A strong need exists to assert a sense of identity separate from the family. A desire to express oneself differently from one's family is a form of trying to attain autonomy. Age thirteen is just the beginning of acquiring a mature sense of autonomy and identity and for some this first attempt could create a crisis in identity.

The Saturn opposition at age fourteen follows at a time that limits again become apparent. Puberty brings with it a set of realities, a leap of maturation, and the need to acquire another set of social and personal responsibilities. Guilt and self-consciousness can accompany this phase. Childhood is over. At age fifteen Jupiter's profile again predominates, and this age brings in a new level of social relationships.

At age eighteen the safety of home is left behind. Pulling up roots is a rite of passage in an attempt to separate one's life and view from the rest of the world, and especially that of one's family. Belief systems that are different have an appeal, especially if they differ from those of the family of origin.

From ages twenty-one through twenty-four a more stable period enters in which it becomes important to try to fit into a particular culture or society. Some get locked into patterns of behavior or a career and family path that has few exits. In these years a search for identity again can be strong. Having a sense of belonging to a group at work, among peer groups, or in community fashions, an ideal of self.

By ages twenty-seven through twenty-nine a period of disillusionment can set in. The goals and beliefs of a decade that were driven by belief in self will no longer work. This is a transitional time, a collapse of the old, sometimes accompanied by turmoil and crisis before a re-visioning of one's life finally takes shape.

The foregoing analysis begins its reference at age two with the Mars return. However, so much of what is now known about development begins much earlier, from birth to age two. The first two to three years of life are the formative ones when enduring psychological patterns are created for a lifetime. Counseling astrologer and family therapist Glennys

Lawton[12], in her work with the Moon and childhood development, associates early attachment patterns with lunar aspects to outer planets, both by birth placement and by transit. The transiting Moon is an important indicator of enduring effects of early childhood because, over the course of the first three months of life, the Moon will make every aspect by transit to the natal chart that it will later make by progression. This illustrates that through astrology it can be determined how an individual will respond to life in later years and how this response will have had its roots in the earliest months of development.

Growth in astrological time frames can correlate with stages in Erik Erikson's lifespan theory of development. Erik Erikson (1902-1994) was a child psychologist and the first to propose a stage theory that went well beyond adolescence and early adulthood. Erikson widened the scope of psychological development from the previous focus on biological drives (Sigmund Freud's psychosexual development) to social and cultural contexts for growth. He believed in the universality of his stages—that they apply to all cultures, saying that although different cultures vary, the underlying structures that govern natural maturation are the same all over the world. Erickson's eight stages are: trust, autonomy, initiative, industry, identity, intimacy, generativity, and ego integrity. There are important concepts in Erikson's theory that link it to current thinking about development. The first is that development is hierarchical; early structures in one stage are assimilated into new structures in the next stage. Second, each stage has its own epoch of development, its developmental apex, but highlights abilities that continue to mature over the entire lifespan. Third, development is qualitatively different at each level. And finally, Erikson's theory includes the social and cultural environment as players in the process of growth.

There is an astrological model of development that correlates astrology with a lifespan theory. It was formulated by astrologer and psychotherapist Glenn Perry, Ph.d.[13] Based upon Erikson's eight stages of man, it has twelve stages, one for each sign of the zodiac. This theory assigns to each sign a phase of individual maturation, an "ascendancy," or peak expression of features of growth, from infancy through the lifespan. The following is a table of this model listing each stage by sign, duration, and developmental objective:

Sign	Duration	Developmental Objective
Aries	Birth to 18 months	Autonomy
Taurus	18 months to 4 years	Object constancy
Gemini	4 years to 7 years	Factual knowledge
Cancer	7 years to 12 years	Emotional security
Leo	12 years to 18 years	Identity, self esteem
Virgo	18 years to 26 years	Competency
Libra	26 years to 35 years	Social relatedness

Scorpio	35 years to 45 years	Transformation
Sagittarius	45 years to 56 years	Wisdom
Capricorn	56 years to 68 years	Authority
Aquarius	68 years to 80 years	Perspective
Pisces	80 years and beyond	Transcendence

Traditional models in psychology and astrology are similar in their understanding of important and predictable periods of growth. However, there are differences as well. First, the trajectory of development in astrology is different from that of psychology. It is cyclical not linear. Additionally, in astrological sequencing a planet may change its angular relationship to other positions in the chart, but it does not alter the essence of its structure. Transiting Saturn retains the same identifiable signature of Saturnian development whether it is in its first square, opposition, or final square to its natal position.

Although influenced by contact with other planets, Saturn's developmental purpose is expressed symbolically and in life in a continuous progression of its essential role: to build one's life through sustained efforts, endured challenges, application of skills, and realistic appraisal of experience. The cycle of Jupiter, wherever it is in its revolution, still retains its basic identity. Whether Jupiter is sextile to its natal position or trine its natal position, or returned, its influence on human growth is always the same.

Dane Rudhyar said, "Each cycle could be considered the lifespan of one specific type of entity retaining specific characteristics, biological or psycho-spiritual, during the entire cycle."[14] In developmental psychology, stages are qualitatively different. They do not resemble each other even though they are connected to the same kind of maturation. For example, it is not one kind of cognitive capacity that changes and grows over time. There are different kinds of cognitive capacities that emerge on a continuum—concrete operations to formal operations—that are structurally different and associated with different strengths and weaknesses and times in life.

In astrology the initial moment of birth holds the key to self-actualization. But this self-actualization, represented by planets in the birth chart, is not a promised fact. The realm of manifestation is one of possibility, not one of literal outcome. Cyclical development in astrology evolves in phases of cycles, but these phases are symbolic, representing multi-level meanings of growth, not absolutes.

Growth in astrology, as in psychology, is expressed in discontinuity, meaning in qualitatively different steps, when the signs from Aries through Pisces are seen as an abstract model of development. This is how human development is depicted in Glenn Perry's model for the lifespan, from the earliest stage under the province of Aries to the last stage under the rulership of Pisces. Whether for the lifespan or for a twenty-seven and a third year cycle, development aligns in a sequence of growth in which characteristically different experiences emerge under each sign's governance. While each sign necessitates the assimilation of learning from the sign before, each is its own whole and not less than the sign before in its contribution to the maturation process.

In psychology the first months of life after birth are important because whatever happens in these early months indelibly influences life thereafter, for better or for worse. From a scientific view, the living moment of birth is not a symbol of potential as it is in astrology, where one symbol contains the whole that will unfold. The moment of birth as understood in psychology is the unformed future, not the seed that contains it. It is the unformed future because the future has yet to be fashioned by the effects of primary relationships on genetic imprints. Genetic predisposition may hold a key to the future, but primary relationships and environmental conditions influence how intrinsic maturation transpires.

Stage theories provide a format for comparing astrology and developmental psychology. There is a richer vocabulary, however, when an assessment of development includes the effects of primary relationships and environmental conditions on biologically predetermined stages of growth. In fact, with recent discoveries in neuroscience, it is this very combination of stage theories and social/relational theories that have contributed to a new understanding of development. The lunar return model blends this new understanding into its theory.

Chapter Three

The Moon and Dyadic Processes of Growth

After remaining unchanged for more than a century, polarized views of development as either an individual process along an intrinsic map of growth or an individual process influenced by relational and environmental conditions have been completely overturned. Out of the recent explosion of brain research and the discovery of the evolutionary substrata of development, psychologists have integrated a new understanding of human growth. The important news in developmental psychology is that many processes of human development that are biologically predetermined *can only be realized through relationships.*

This discovery was derived from more than a decade of infant research and infant/parent dyad research. Since the 1990s, advanced technology using PET (positron emission tomography) and MRI (magnetic resonance imaging) brain scan imaging as well as frame-by-frame filming of interactions between infants and parents have illuminated micro-processes of relational connectedness that influence individual growth.[1] As a result of these observations, information has flooded the field of developmental psychology with scientific evidence that crucial aspects of development cannot take place outside of relational exchanges.

Development is co-created by two people. It is not a one-person process but a two-person process. Because of the effect of relationships on bio-genetic and evolutionary structures of the brain, stages of development can only be activated in the matrix of relationship—interpersonal or inter-environmental.

Development is experience dependent, not just at the psychological level but at the level of genes, neuron circuitry, brain chemistry (including endocrine functioning), and brain structure.[2] The brain, which is the most unformed organ of the body at birth, requires the attunement of a relationship in order to mature.[3]

The idea that development is influenced by the experience of relationship sounds simple but it is really complex. Also, it may sound like a restatement of a familiar postulate of the major psychoanalytic theories of the twentieth century: that early parental relationships shape enduring features of psychological development. In fact, for nearly a century, most models of development in psychology have recognized that parental relationships play major roles in early development.

What is new and different here is that development is co-created through relationships. It is not just influenced by a relationship but co-created at the level of brain structure and neuron circuitry. The brain at birth overproduces neuron receptors that sit in states of readiness to be connected through interactive emotional processes between mother and infant.

There are biologically predetermined time frames during which certain regulatory functions must be set. These correspond to stages of development in stage theories. However, in order for development to jump along the continuum of stages of growth, emotional exchanges between mother (or primary caregiver) and infant or child must create a "readiness" for action.

Many metabolic and physiological processes associated with stages of development, such as emotional and cognitive maturation and the ability to regulate states of stress, are dependent upon specific relational exchanges between mother and child for adaptive functioning. After a time-sensitive period (generally within the first eighteen to twenty-four months) has elapsed, a pruning[4] of the overabundance of neurons that were present at birth takes place, and excess neurons that were not wired together within the first eighteen months begin to scale back. "Neurons that wire together, fire together[5]" in sets of complex interactions that form the basis for cognitive and emotional maturation.

Development is experience-dependent at the level of genes as well. Genes have two functions: they are templates for information that are passed down through generations and they have a transcription function. Genetic transcriptions are based upon the codes in DNA sequences and are the rules that determine which proteins are to be synthesized by which cells.

What has been recently discovered is that the transcription function of genes is *both preprogrammed and experience dependent*. Experience determines when preprogrammed genes synthesize proteins. This is a very different concept from the belief in the immutable construct of the genetic code. "A wide range of studies now confirms that development is a product of the effect of experience on genetic potential."[6] Sequences that are open for input are then programmed for emotional and psychobiological development through early relational exchanges.

Extensive research has also confirmed[6] that it is the earliest relationship with the primary caregiver, usually but not necessarily the mother, that catalyzes the internal unfolding of development. But the experience in infancy of all early relationships, father and grandparents as well as mother, help create development that sets the stage for many aspects of life that follow. Relationships co-construct internal neurobiological structures that become the adaptive (or maladaptive) response systems of emotion, cognition, and physiological sensitivity and functioning for a lifetime. In fact, in the last few years, research in neuroplasticity confirms that relationships and the environment can continue to shape the physical structure of the brain and its wiring long into adulthood.[7]

There is reciprocity between development that has been preset by biological clocks and that is dependent on nurturing communication. The fact that much of the maturation process is biologically pre-set is not disputed. In fact there is evidence that a mother's instinct to nurture her infant, which in turn catalyzes hormones in the child, is driven by the biological production of hormones in her body in a system created by evolution long ago. There are time-sensitive periods all throughout childhood that are genetically predetermined. But biological maturation requires transactions between mother and child to become activated. So the question of nature versus nurture is moot; nature requires nurture to implement its resources. Of course many genetic, environmental, and social conditions outside of the primary relational matrix do influence human growth. This is also undeniable. But then the capacity to manage all kinds of external or even genetic influences is very much determined by the quality of emotional attunement that occurs in the primary relationship.

The key concept, therefore, that has surfaced and now underlies current awareness in developmental psychology is that there are open systems of development that influence cognitive and emotional functioning, as well as to the ability to regulate stress. These open systems of development are relationship dependent. Human growth is a two-person, not a one-person, phenomenon. It is co-created by two people, mother and infant, in a mutual system of communication, and what is co-created becomes encoded in the neural network of the infants' developing mind.

The reason that this relational principle of development is so significant here is that the Moon in astrology represents emotional development through the primary relationship. In astrology the Moon at birth can be interpreted as an indicator of the quality of both the earliest attachment and the earliest inter-subjective experiences. Attachment refers to the bio-psychological need of every child for protection and security. The nature of the security system that the mother provides for the child very early in the child's life will have enduring effects on the way emotional security is experienced for a lifetime. Inter-subjectivity refers to both the verbal and non-verbal communication that is created between mother and child that allows them to know each others intent and feelings. This communication is unique to their system alone. Attachment and inter-subjective connectedness are related but different because, in theory, it is possible to feel a secure sense of attachment to one's parent without having depth of meaningful exchange. Inter-subjectivity gives meaning to interactions[8] and with it the mother can convey a contingent (approximate but good enough) understanding of her child's emotional states.

Much has been written in the literature of astrology about the Moon. It is associated with the feminine principal that operates in concert with the Sun, the yin to the yang. It is the emotional and receptive component of nature and the part of self that interacts with the strivings of the Sun to fulfill the soul's destiny.

Mythical images relate the Moon to the archetypal mother, the nurturer, the container, and the healer of the universe. It presides over darkness, mystery, insanity, menses, the womb, and fluids. The Moon represents the need for closeness, for warmth, for security, physical and emotional, as well as dependency needs in general.

In the literature of psychological astrology [9], the Moon represents the individual and the mother, and the quality of nurturing and attachment in this primary relationship. In its birth sign, and in aspect with other planets in the natal chart, the Moon represents the need for nurturing, the type of nurturing that is most desired, and the way in which this need is met or not met in the primary relationship. For example, a Moon at birth in Taurus might explain the child's need for tangible security, financial or material, that provides an experience of being nurtured. Aspects to the natal Moon in Taurus further describe the nature of the relationship with a primary caregiver who was or was not able to provide the needed experience of emotional security.

The Moon contains a component that is both one's self and one's mother, combined. It therefore can be called a self-other configuration, meaning that both the individual (self) and the mother (other) are merged into one symbol. This one symbol, the Moon, describes how development is created in mutual interactions of emotional exchange. In its birth sign the Moon represents the nature of the interlocking psychic worlds of mother and child. The Moon in aspect to other planets in the birth chart renders a specific picture of an individual's internalized relationship with the mother that continues to press for and recreate the original model of nurturing in other relationships throughout life.

In its specific sign, house, and aspect placement at birth, the Moon can describe how the mother's life, nature, and relationship with her child influences the child's emotional nature. It represents the way a mother behaves toward her child in accordance with how she perceives him and how the child in turn is affected by her behavior. It is bi-directional. If, for example, the child's Moon at birth is in Capricorn, the mother could be fearful of rejection or emotionally rigid, but perceives her child to be emotionally guarded. As a result she withdraws from her child. Her withdrawal creates an anxiety in the child and serves as negative feedback that verifies that her child is indeed lacking in love for her. This becomes a mutual system that has been co-created, and the child's inability to regulate anxiety could likely result.

In addition, an aspect between the Moon and another planet can explain the emotional world of both child and mother. In this case the relationship is governed by the qualities ascribed to the planet that aspects the Moon. A Moon-Pluto conjunction could describe a jealous, manipulative, or controlling mother or it could describe the child's need to be secretive or to control emotional expression because the mother was either secretive, or even the opposite—because her emotions were cruel, invasive or eruptive. Again, it is bi-directional. The Moon in aspect with another planet could also describe a splitting of two parts of an individual psyche. This is especially evident when the Moon opposes another planet.

A natal Moon in opposition to Uranus could reflect both the internalized self and the internalized mother at odds with each other. The internalized mother refers to the relationship with the mother that has had a psychological impact on the child. The Moon reflects the part of self that needs intimacy and nurturing, and Uranus reflects the part of self that disrupts bonds and does not want to be committed to emotional connections. This opposition could represent the child's conflict with emotional intimacy as a result of an insecure attachment to his mother.

The Moon's sign and aspects can suggest how a mother's real life experience is passed down to her child. The Moon in Taurus might describe a mother's experience of safety and security in her life that she in turn passes along to her child.

Because the Moon is the symbol for matrilineal descent, the sign can describe a multi-generational transmission process[10]—the inheritance of either unresolved personal experiences passed down for generations or of personality traits passed along the matrilineal line of descent. For instance, a woman with the Moon conjunct Jupiter in Pisces in the fourth house might come from a family in which the mothers over generations are caregivers, not just of their immediate family, but also of their extended family.

A Moon that is square Jupiter could describe an emotional imbalance, or a tendency to excess and indulgence in the mother that is passed down to the child who in turn goes through emotional highs and lows—states similar to the imbalances of an emotionally unstable mother.

In these ways characteristic inheritance is revealed in the chart by either the sign of the natal Moon or a planet in aspect to the natal Moon. Either can challenge a child with the same problem that her mother was unable to resolve.

Liz Greene, renowned astrologer and a director of the Centre for Psychological Astrology, notes: "Your Moon sign shows something about how you experience or see your mother. It describes your feeling nature." Gloria Star, professional astrologer, author, and teacher, explains that the sign of the Moon reveals the way in which the child perceives the mother. "It makes no difference whether the mother sees herself in this light or not. The child holds these particular perceptions of her because she is projecting her own inner needs for security onto her. As the child masters adulthood, these perceptions determine how that individual will play the nurturing/mothering role."[11]

But the sign of the natal Moon and aspects to other planets can also describe the real relationship between mother and child, not just the child's projection onto the mother of inner needs or fantasies. In other words, it can describe the actual quality of the mother and child attachment relationship. It reveals the way the mother responds to a child's specific needs and the way the child adopts a default expression of emotional needs for a lifetime.

A Moon in Gemini at birth, for example, implies that something about the attachment relationship fostered the child's need for clear perception, for information, and for communication. The need to be heard and to be understood as a result of the relationship with mother becomes a paramount need. Perhaps something about the mother's story or form of communication either enlightened or confused the child, or perhaps something about their relationship encouraged the child to love to read, write, and communicate.

The Moon in Pisces at birth might describe the way the attachment relationship sensitized a child's identification with loss or suffering. It might describe difficulty experiencing psychological boundaries because the mother's emotional or physical needs were overwhelming.

All the above interpretations of the Moon's sign and aspects at birth have validity. The range of possible meanings is evidence of the complexity of the interpenetration of psyches between mother and child.

The following is a table with general descriptions for each natal Moon sign. This chart specifically describes the enduring effect of the primary relationship on attachment and inter-subjective needs of the child. These descriptions are possible manifestations, their exact nature being dependent upon many other variables in the individual's life.

Moon in Birth Signs Representing the Effect of the Primary Relationship on Expression of Emotional Needs or Conditions for Love

Birth Moon in Aries	Effect: Need to go it alone, to be one's own person, have self-reliance
Birth Moon in Taurus	Effect: Need for tangible security is paramount
Birth Moon in Gemini	Effect: Need for communication, to be heard, and to be understood
Birth Moon in Cancer	Effect: Need to be taken care of, and/or to care for others
Birth Moon in Leo	Effect: Need for self-expression, to be seen in order to feel special, loved
Birth Moon in Virgo	Effect: Need to get the job done right, be of service, be perfect, correct the flaws
Birth Moon in Libra	Effect: Need for relationship to feel validated, to accommodate the feelings of others
Birth Moon in Scorpio	Effect: Need to insure survival, protect, get beneath the surface, find the hidden truth
Birth Moon in Sagittarius	Effect: Need to be freed from restrictions, to not feel constrained
Birth Moon in Capricorn	Effect: Need to overcome insecurity and fear of rejection, need to gain external respect to achieve internal security
Birth Moon in Aquarius	Effect: Need for emotional distance, objectivity, and freedom to be independent, to follow one's unique dream or calling
Birth Moon in Pisces	Effect: Need to feel united with and to identify with the feelings of others, or lose oneself in others

The sign opposite the Moon sign at birth is an equally important signifier of the effect of the primary relationship on attachment experiences and the capacity for inter-subjective relating. This sign is a shadow sign, the implied but unstated and yet ever-present relationship exerting its influence. The Moon as a symbol of two people in relationship to each other holds the archetype of Aries and Libra in astrological opposition.

Opposites co-exist in nature to balance and counter-balance forces within a system. Matter and anti-matter in physics[12], heliocentric and geocentric positions in astronomy[13], and tensegrity[14] in the structure of molecules in biology are all examples of systems with opposing and counteractive forces that maintain the architecture of their inherent designs.

These counterbalancing forces exist in astrology in the birth sign of the Moon and the sign opposing it. Even if the opposite sign never appears in the chart, it is an implied reaction to, or complementary of, the birth Moon. Every Moon sign involves its opposite. While the variations in interpretation are manifold, here are some interpretations for this assumed opposition implied in the Moon's position at birth:

Moon in Aries in reaction to Libra: the need to be individuated from dependency needs and relationship with mother.

Moon in Taurus in reaction to Scorpio: the need for security as a result of crisis in mother's history or in the family lineage.

Moon in Gemini in reaction to Sagittarius: the need for communication, to be heard because of lack of focus from mother.

Moon in Cancer in reaction to Capricorn: the need for emotional security because of an experience of parental rejection

Moon in Leo in reaction to Aquarius: the need for recognition and admiration from a detached or unavailable parent.

Moon in Virgo in reaction to Pisces: the need to be rational, level headed, because of over emotional or worried parent.

Moon in Libra in reaction to Aries: the need for emotional balance and connection because of separation from primary relationship.

Moon in Scorpio in reaction to Taurus: the need for survival skills because of lack of secure attachment.

Moon in Sagittarius in reaction to Gemini: the need for the truth because of lack of information or unspoken communication.

Moon in Capricorn in reaction to Cancer: the need for approval from parent; need to parent emotional mother.

Moon in Aquarius in reaction to Leo: the need to detach from drama of mother or family.

Moon in Pisces in reaction to Virgo: the need to save mother from illness or disability

These are examples of how energies of the manifest sign of the Moon at birth and its shadow opposite are balanced and counterbalanced in the primary relationship. The interpretations above assume that opposing signs are reactive to birth signs, but complimentary interpretations could be accurate as well.

"Under the light of the Moon, relationships have their cycles, family life has its cycles, and so too does history. There is nothing new under the Sun because the Moon has done it all before. This cyclical experience of life is really a psychological state of being. We might call it matriarchal, because it is a vision of life that is essentially female and organic, reflecting the processes of conception, pregnancy, birth, puberty, maturation, aging, and dying."[15]

Chapter Four

Theoretical Foundations for the Lunar Return Model of Development

Three theories provide the psychological underpinnings for the lunar return model of development: attachment theory, interpersonal theory, and interpersonal neurobiology. These theories have contributed to the current understanding of the role of emotional connection in early development.

John Bowlby's attachment theory[1] attributes the capacity for, and quality of, intimacy in adult relationships to the kind of attachment and bonding between child and mother in the first few years of the child's life.

Daniel Stern's Interpersonal Theory[2] reveals the intersubjective nature of development of the self through very early communication patterns between infant and mother.

Daniel Siegle's Interpersonal neurobiology[3] is the product of the interdisciplinary study of neuroscience and psychology which he developed with Allan Schore, and other research and clinical psychologists.

John Bowlby's Theory of Attachment
Attachment theory has its roots in ethology and the observation that natural selection favored mammals that protected their young and responded to their infants needs for security. Attachment behavior appears to have had an evolutionary function. It is common to all mammals across all cultures and all time, and throughout history every child by seven to eught months of age becomes attached to a primary caregiver. There is never a question of

whether a child becomes attached to a primary caregiver because a child will attach to whoever is the most consistent caregiver. The quality of the attachment, however, can vary, dependent upon the nature of the bond between child and caregiver. A child can, for example, be securely attached to the parent, or can be insecurely attached, and there are many variations of the latter. Anxious resistant, avoidant, and disorganized attachments are the three general classifications of insecure attachments, and disorganized attachments have been identified as most predictive of emotional disorders. What is important about an attachment classification, however, is that it is not a description of a person, it is a description of a relationship.

Although John Bowlby, the British psychoanalyst who developed this theory, was primarily focused on understanding the nature of the infant-caregiver relationship, he believed that attachment characterizes human experience from "the cradle to the grave." Research on adult attachment supports the hypothesis that the form of attachment that was prominent in childhood will have profound effects on all relationships, including adult romantic relationships, throughout a lifetime.[4]

Daniel Stern's Interpersonal World of the Infant
Daniel Stern, M.D., professor of psychiatry at the University of Geneva and Cornell Medical School, originally presented his theory in 1985. It is about the non-verbal, right brain, and implicit level of communication that takes place between mother and child. Dr. Stern altered the understanding of development and the infant's role in this process. His research confirmed that in normal development the infant is not a passive by-stander but an active participant in its own development. The infant brings, even at the very beginning of life, many facial, gestural, and vocal signals that enter into the communication and response system with the mother, that build a sense of self. In Stern's model there are four "domains of self" that consolidate within the first fifteen to eighteen months of life to form a sense of self. These are the emergent self, the core self, the inter-subjective self, and the verbal self.[5] There are many variations in how and when a specific domain develops, depending upon the child, the relationship to its mother or primary caregiver, the environment, or genetic influences. Even though they are not age- or stage-specific, the domains of development do come online sequentially and once active they do not stop but continuously develop throughout the lifetime.

Daniel Siegle's Interpersonal Neurobiology
Interpersonal neurobiology, formulated by Daniel Siegle, M.D. of UCLA's Department of Psychiatry and Center for Interdisciplinary Studies, is based upon the latest research in neuroscience and developmental psychology. Evidence confirms that human development, on the level of brain structure itself, is experience dependent. It is dependent on the emo-

tional communication, largely non-verbal, between mother and infant in the first two years of life. The mother's capacity to adequately regulate her child's immature coping mechanisms activates bio-behavioral growth that emerges in the developmental stages associated with many models of stage development. Stages of development require the release of certain hormones that can only be activated through a relationship. The mother's attunement to her child's needs, both for stimulation and for comfort, acts on the neurobiological chemistry of the infant to release these chemicals and hormones that proceed to connect the neuro-circuitry of the brain in optimal ways so that cognitive and emotional functioning can mature.

Interpersonal neurobiology inspires new forms of psychotherapy to enhance the relational awareness of the therapist and client. It holds the belief, and the research to back this belief, that the healing relationship has the capacity of both psychotherapist and patient and to alter the brain chemistry and to create new neuron circuits.[6]

In the lunar return model of development, the Moon describes a similar dyadic process of development that John Bowlby, Daniel Stern, and Dan Siegle depict in their theories of attachment, intersubjectivity, and interpersonal neurobiology.

In astrology, the Moon's position at birth tells the story of mutual attunement between mother and child, and the result this has on the emotional characteristics of the child for an entire lifetime. Because the Moon in astrology is the symbol for nurturing and being nurtured, it represents the experience-dependent, relational nature of growth. The Moon's position imparts an understanding of the effects of relationship on an individual's overall development. This is reflected not just in its birth position but also in its secondary progressed placements.

In its progressed placements, the sign of the Moon provides a code for understanding what aspect of development is being challenged and what kind of life experience it can fulfill. The Moon continues to symbolize a relational system as it progresses from birth through the sequence of signs in the zodiac.

The cycle of the secondary progressed Moon is different from any other secondary progression. It is the only secondary progressed planet that travels through all twelve signs of the zodiac by the time Saturn returns to its birth position at approximately age thirty. One needs the full lunar experience in order to be prepared for the Saturn return.

The progressed Moon is also the only secondary progressed planet that can cycle around the chart up to three times in a lifetime. In this regard it resembles a transit cycle. Yet it is not a transit. It functions both like a progression and a transit because it has characteristics of both. In a general way it can be interpreted as both the unfolding of internal emotional maturity (progressions) and the manifestation of external pressures on this internal process (transits).

The Moon in astrology is the holder of memory. Rupert Sheldrake, the British molecular biologist and author of *The Habits of Nature*[7] introduced the concept of the bio-morphic field. This refers to the hypothesis that anything living has a biological energy field that sustains itself over time through resonance with its past.

Like biological fields, the Moon or any planet in the astrology chart has a bio-metaphysical field. And in the same way that biological fields carry memory, the Moon carries memory of its past, and its energy field can continue over time because it resonates with its past.

The transiting Moon travels through one sign about every two and a half days of life and is the only planet that travels through all twelve signs every month.

The transiting Moon foreshadows the course of the secondary progressed Moon. Any aspect to a natal planet that the Moon makes by transit during the first months of life, it will later make by secondary progression. This is how the transiting Moon foretells all emotional experience for a lifetime in the very first months of life. And this is how relational and emotional processes that are evoked under the influence of the secondary progressed Moon carry the memory of their past.

The Moon represents memory and memory is everywhere in the brain, not just in one location. The transiting Moon vitalizes patterns in the chart that will later be remembered under the influence of the secondary progressed Moon. And then the secondary progressed Moon will create memories that are awakened again in its cycles around the chart every twenty-seven and a third years, up to three times in a lifespan.

With every lunar return, the developmental journey begins again and the same aspects to natal positions that were contacted in a previous cycle will be contacted again.

Memory that is evoked through resonance with past states may be conscious or unconscious, but either way it can provide incentive to redo and redeem the past.

An enormous body of research in psychology has been conducted that confirms that development is co-created in the context of relationship.

Early social environment, mediated by the mother or primary caregiver, directly shapes the structures of the brain that have been created through the history of evolution. There are some important differences, however, between developmental psychology and astrology with regard to understanding this co-creational principle.

Astrologers would not say that the primary relationship between mother and infant *creates or activates* development that is mirrored in the patterns in the horoscope. To the contrary, astrologers would say the opposite. In astrology, patterns of development pre-exist living relationship and already describe a range of features that could manifest in the living relationship between mother and child. The process of potential fulfillment is inscribed in the symbols of the chart itself and seeks realization through many experiences, including primary relationships with parents. Cycles that are set in motion from the moment of birth depict the evolution of this process. These cycles have a life of their own and are not seen as experience or relationship dependent.

Relationships, astrologers would contend, are players in the script. They help actualize and fulfill something that exists *a priori*, before birth. They do not initiate or set in motion life's developmental journey.

Some astrologers differ in how much they feel the quality of life is already a given, predetermined by the metaphysical signatures at birth, and how much the quality of life is determined in real time, the clients' living experience, which co-constructs the meaning of preexisting astrological symbols. Most astrologers are not literalists, or at least they do not intend to be literalists. Astrologers are educated about the laws of indeterminacy and the many ways patterns in a chart can be realized. They recognize that spontaneity plays an important role in shaping the way an individual will activate the potential of his horoscope even though the patterns themselves are givens.

Yet the idea that what occurs is co-created through relationships is not embraced in astrological symbols. The very nature of the art we practice binds us to some degree to the epistemology of pre-determinism. We must operate within a frame of reference that has already been established even if there is latitude for interpretation.

Similar to the pre-determinism of psychological stage theories and genetic directives that derived from DNA at the dawn of civilization[8], astrological patterns for each life come from their own distant source, as pre-coded scripts that unfold in timed sequences, although cyclical and not linear, along a stipulated course of development. If astrologers embrace the current definition of development, then astrological patterns and cycles, like the genetic code, are the givens that still need to be actualized through relationships.

What can be seen in the chart is an individual's potential in the abstract that can be released and co-created through experience and living relationships. And depending upon the nature of an individual's experience or relationships, the potential described by the patterns in the chart can be maximized or truncated.

Rather than interpreting relationships as players in a script that has already been written in the chart, relationships, by this new experience dependent definition of development, are the catalysts of the chart.

Therefore the Moon is not an encapsulated air tight representation unfolding in time and space. It represents internal development that is dependent upon the living external environment to activate its inherent potential. Inherent potential is archetypally[9] configured in the chart through the symbols and planetary configurations. But the ability to realize the potential of these archetypes is mediated through dyadic interactions of real relationships.

The Moon embodies the nature/nurture dependency theme. The Moon decodes nature's developmental trajectory through its symbol and sign and simultaneously requires nurture of a living and spontaneous relationship to fulfill its symbolic promise.

The Moon is an astrological placement that bridges the divide between the definition of human development in astrology and the definition of development in current psychology.

This signature of the Moon holds the key for co-mingling astrology with the now accepted relational definition of development because the Moon is the symbol of development through the relationship.

While any symbol in a chart can be activated through one's inter-relationship with the environment or another person, the Moon gives the most interpretive access to the purpose and nature of human growth as it is understood in the developmental sciences today.

Chapter Five

The Lunar Return Model of Development: Span of Attachment

The developmental model that is proposed here is based upon a three-part hypothesis. The first part is that the signs of the zodiac correspond to developmental stages in psychology. The second is that the Moon conveys how the sequence and meaning of developmental stages unfold through the signs of the zodiac, each of which is twenty-seven and a third years. This is the length of time it takes the Moon to travel through all twelve signs to complete its lunar return. And the third part of this hypothesis is that the repetitive cycles of the progressed Moon can bring resolution to the issues presented in earlier cycles.

The symbol of the Moon itself captures the essence of human development as it is understood today: that it is formed by relational exchanges. The Moon is a representation of the two-person process of maturation. It is the symbol of emotional and cognitive development that takes place within and because of relationships. It is the symbol of the convergence of nature and nurture, of being and experience, depending on impinging conditions from within or without. There is a relational necessity for growth. Whether this relational component is with another person, an ideal, one's community, or external events, the Moon represents the capacity to catalyze this growth. The Moon, from its position at birth (sign, house, and aspect patterns) travels on a developmental trajectory that is always affected by relationships.

The lunar return model of development is first based upon the premise that the signs of the zodiac correspond to phases of development observed and researched in psychology.

Second, it is based upon the premise that the Moon, as it progresses through the signs, conveys this developmental information. Third is that the developmental pathway is twenty-seven and a third years, the exact amount of time it takes the Moon by secondary progression to return to the position it occupied at birth. And fourth, it is based upon the premise that the developmental pathway is not linear as it is portrayed in traditional psychology, but circular, from birth to the first lunar return and then around again, up to three times in a lifespan. Each time the Moon goes around, there is an opportunity to revisit and even revise ways of responding to difficult life circumstances.

The lunar return model of development utilizes the sign of the Moon both in its birth position and in its secondary progressed positions. The secondary progressed Moon carries developmental information around the zodiac and the same developmental themes that emerge during the first twenty-seven and a third years of life are repeated in the second and even third cycles around the chart. The first cycle is the formative one that reveals the effects of early relationships on emotional and cognitive development. The progressed Moon's movement through each sign and house around the chart in subsequent cycles illustrates how development is both rooted in the past yet ongoing into adulthood and older age.

This theory uses the tropical zodiac and secondary progressions. Other systems would not work as well to illustrate this theory. Any system, for example, in which the meaning of a sign is not as important as the meaning of a planet would not impart the same information. Also, any system in which the Moon progresses at the same rate as the Sun, as in solar arc directions (about a degree a year) would not work in this particular model. While the Moon in any system of astrology has developmental meaning, the secondary progressed Moon travels about thirteen to fourteen degrees in a year, so it moves quickly through the signs of the zodiac. In doing so, the timing of the first twenty-seven and a third years approximates developmental stages of childhood, adolescence, and early adulthood in developmental psychology.

One way to illustrate that astrological signs are analogous to developmental stages from birth to the end of the first cycle is with the wheel of the zodiac divided into twelve sections. Like an equal twelve-house chart system, each section, or house, is equivalent to approximately two or two and a half years of life and the entire wheel is equivalent to twenty-seven and a half years, the length of time for a lunar return. In this graphic way it is possible to see how stages of development progress (Figure 1).

There are general time frames for stages of growth, windows during which development has a readiness to emerge.[1] Dividing a wheel into twelve stages is an abstract illustration of development. For some stages in this diagram, a two year period is fairly accurate, while for

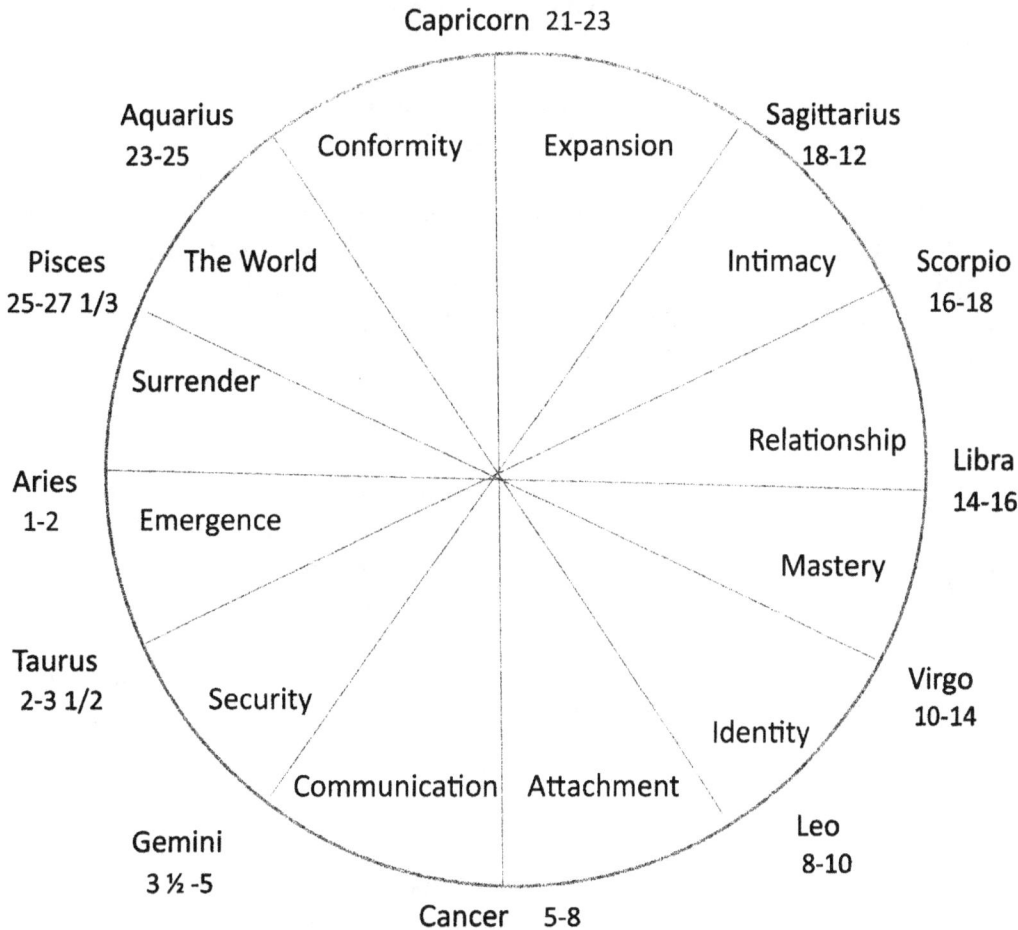

Figure 1. Twelve Stages of Develoment from Birth to Age 27 1/3 Years, the First Lunar Return

others a two and a half year margin is reasonable. But it is not always clear which stages are longer or shorter, give or take a few months, and give or take circumstances unique for every person. So a wheel that divides maturation in the first twenty-seven and a third years into two or two and a half year frames is general. But for the sake of a visual example, the correspondence between signs of the zodiac and developmental stages is clearer when they are divided this way.

The lunar return model represents development that is both continuous and discontinuous. An example of continuous development[2] is physical growth. A person's increased height and weight over time are always measurements of the same thing and are extensions of their own previous states.

Discontinuous development, on the other hand, occurs in sudden leaps from a less mature organization of development to a more sophisticated level of growth that is qualitatively different. "Infant researchers have documented that development occurs in leaps and bounds, and critical periods of bio-behavioral development are accompanied by significant qualitative shifts."[3] The idea here is that a significant qualitative shift occurs, like the caterpillar becoming the butterfly, or creative expression yielding to abstract reasoning, or moral judgment based upon parental punishment changing to one based upon an inner sense of right and wrong. These are all examples of discontinuity in development.

In astrology, development can be represented in both continuous and discontinuous patterns. Continuity of development is recognizable when an outer planet cycles through changing phases on its way around the zodiac and every phase retains the characteristic of the planet. No matter what phase transiting Saturn is in, for instance, it never loses its Saturn identity. Similarly, in the lunar return model, development is continuous in the cycle of the Moon. It goes around once, and then repeats and builds on itself, but is always about the meaning of growth through the symbol of the Moon. Additionally, this theory is continuous because it is multi-linear. Like Daniel Stern's interpersonal theory of development, once a capacity of self is present, it is not supplanted by a more evolved kind of growth, but continues to mature on its own course even as other capacities emerge. In this lunar return model of growth, each sign represents a capacity of self that continues on its own developmental trajectory, never lost, even as the next sign appears in the forefront.

The lunar model of development is also discontinuous in that from one sign to the next, Aries through Pisces, a leap occurs from one kind of growth to the next that is completely unique from the preceding form. No sign is more important than another, or less evolved than another. All twelve signs represent modes of growth that are on the same par, just different. Taurus is not the next level up the developmental sequence after Aries. Rather, it is the next sign, with its own distinct context of growth that operates concurrently with the maturational achievements represented by the sign of Aries. Perhaps some growth in the Taurus phase is dependent upon the achievements of Aries, but it is not more advanced than Aries. And the capacities associated with Taurus, as with any astrological sign, will continue to evolve even after the next stage, in this example Gemini, comes online.

The twelve signs of the zodiac can be seen as stages of development. From Aries through Pisces, these stages represent twelve types of psychological and spiritual mastery. They characterize both distinct stages of development from birth to to the end of the first cycle as well as continuity of development even though the emphasis may shift to another kind of maturation.

A feature of correlating developmental phases with astrological signs is that for every sign that parallels a developmental phase, the sign opposite plays just as important a role in the outcome. This phenomenon of corresponding opposites was depicted in the previous chapter with the sign of the birth Moon and its opposing sign. So in the lunar return model as well, development is represented by the relationship between each sign to its opposite.

The twelve signs are divided into three spans. The first span, from Aries through Cancer, is the span of attachment. The second, from Leo through Scorpio, is the span of relationship. And the third, from Sagittarius through Pisces, is the span of the world.

The Span of Attachment—Aries through Cancer
Attachment refers to the experience of security and protection in the primary relationship. In the first phase of life, attachment is said to be "in the making,"[4] meaning it does not happen instantly. But by the eighth month of the first year of life, the attachment relationship between child and mother is formed[5].

Aries, the first sign of the zodiac, represents the first stage from birth to age two in the Span of Attachment. Aries is the sign of initiation, of beginning something new. In developmental psychology, specifically in Daniel Stern's Interpersonal Theory, the first phase describes exactly that state of initiation[6]. It is called the domain of the emergent self. The understanding is that in emerging, the infant is not a passive recipient but an active participant in its own growth and in communication with its mother. In addition, Aries in the physical body represents the head, and rapid neurological changes take place in these early months. Many functions of the brain, specifically emotional, cognitive, and the ability to regulate stress, are still unformed at birth. They mature only through the relationship with a primary caregiver whose sensitivity to the needs of her child becomes encoded in networks of the infant's maturing brain. But the growth of the infant is dependent on its mother and therefore, there first must be a relationship in order for there to be a self[6]. The success of this Aries phase, then, is dependent upon a Libra experience, a relationship, and one that is nurturing and attuned to the infant.

Taurus is the next stage, from approximately ages two to age three and a half. Taurus in astrology represents physical security. In psychology, specifically in Daniel Stern's Interpersonal Theory of development, this is the phase in which psychological security in the attachment relationship can become reasonably predictable and attuned. The core self develops now. The core self is physical, concrete, bounded, and has a sense of continuity over time[7]. It has a sense of where "I end and you begin." Security also depends upon clear and safe boundaries, physical and psychological. Emotions are rooted in the body and the infant's bodily based emotions can easily go out of control in this stage.

Scorpio, the sign of interdependency, is the sign opposite Taurus. It defines dark, intense emotions. The security that is born of Taurus depends upon how Scorpio emotions are managed in the close relationship between parent and child. A parent's capacity to tolerate her child's dark emotions (rage, sadness, hostility) is related to that parent's ability to control her own emotions so they are not unleashed destructively. The parent must differentiate his or her own intense feelings from those of the child who has only an immature capacity to tolerate them. This tolerance for, and differentiation of, intense emotion are factors that help a parent provide clear, safe and consistent boundaries for the toddler.

The third stage in the Span of Attachment is the phase of Gemini. This sign of communication and verbal skill encompasses a time frame from ages three and a half to five. In developmental psychology, again in the Interpersonal Theory of development, the third phase is the domain of the verbal self[8]. However, communication is not a province of this time span alone. Communication, especially right-brain interaction, which is non-verbal and emotional, has been present since infancy. It is left-brain activity that comes online now. The bifurcation of mental processes—right-brain from left-brain—is represented by the sign of Gemini. With left brain activity, the executive functions of the mind develop. One function is the ability for the child to narrate his own story based upon a sense of continuity over time[9]. This ability, however, is not just singular, but plural, because the minds of people have always been linked and their stories have been passed down for eons. There is evidence that the non-verbal right brain, from the beginning of human life on earth, has had the capacity to be in touch with the thoughts of others that are connected to a kind of "world mind"—a Sagittarius experience[10]. This has been accomplished through neuron networks, some called mirror neurons, and some called oscillators,[11] and are part of right brain functions that have connected people to each other for the purpose of survival. Sagittarius signifies the effects of culture on thinking; on perception, cognition, language skills, and memory. The development of mental processes, in the individual child as a result of thousands of years of neural connections has been dependent upon synchronization and integration of the right and left brain.

The fourth stage in the Span of Attachment is Cancer, the sign of attachment and nurturing. In this phase, at ages five and six, it is possible to see how the earliest attachment relationship has become internalized and the child emerges as a person in the world. Attachment systems in the family acquire unique characteristics. All family members contribute to the attachment system. This stage illustrates the function of a genogram,[12] a map of family relationships passed down through generations. Cancer governs the patterns families develop to insure a sense of security and love. Attachment in this Cancer stage, therefore, is not just to mother but to father as well. This is how Cancer's opposite sign, Capricorn, relates to this phase. The support of a father is the number one factor in helping a mother provide a secure base of attachment for her child.[13] The relationship with the father will also be a predictor of relationships with authority figures later in life. The father can provide a model for relating to teachers and other adults outside of the family, who have already entered the child's world. The father can acclimate his child to the world of conditions. This is a time when a child can relinquish more fantasy, about himself and about the world, and begin to see reality more logically.[14] To the extent that he has had a sense of security and love at home, he has more capacity to accept the rules of life, and the reality of his own limits.

These four stages that are divided into approximately two-year segments from birth to age eight could also comprise much shorter time frames. In a concentric wheel of development, like a fractal diagram of a wheel within a wheel, they are analogous to the stages from birth to three years old in Margaret Mahler's Theory of Separation-Individuation[15]. According to Mahler's theory, the length of time it takes a child to attain enough internal security to be able to sustain a separate sense of self is approximately three years. In astrology the Aries phase would be the one in which the child's reference to the world is egocentric and omnipotent. Nothing exists that he or she does not control or initiate into being. In the Taurus phase the first awareness that objects, including mother, are separate entities, creates an intolerable anxiety. There is no object constancy yet, no ability to hold in memory the continuity of mother, that she exists even though she may be temporarily absent. The Gemini phase is equivalent to Mahler's practicing phase, when a child can experience that mother comes and goes and comes back again and is not permanently gone. Through new motor and perceptual skills, the child learns that both child and mother can come and go and return to each other. The Cancer phase represents rapprochement, the phase of full object constancy, when a sense of emotional security is attained because mother has been internalized. In the successful realization of rapprochement, it is possible for a child to balance both a sense of autonomy in separation and the need for dependency on mother's love and nurturing.

The four stages that comprise The Span of Attachment in the lunar return model of development are also reflected in the first four domains in Daniel Stern's Interpersonal Theory of development. These four domains extend from birth through eighteen months of age. According to Stern's extensive research, it takes approximately eighteen months to move from the emergent self, which first appears from birth to three months, to the core self, which first appears at about three to six months, to the beginning of the subjective self, which comes into being any time between nine and twelve months. At about eighteen months, the verbal self emerges. Then all four domains can continue to develop together as a result of the attachment and intersubjective relationship between infant and mother. In astrology these domains can be represented by the signs of Aries through Cancer.

Development witnessed symbolically through the lens of astrology, therefore, has subcycles that reflects the holistic nature of human growth. All aspects of growth—cognitive, emotional, physical—are represented in every cycle and move through the same sequence of signs. It is possible to see stages unfold from birth through eighteen months that correlate with the same sequence of astrological signs, as do stages from birth through age six years. Like concentric circles within circles, or fractals in mathematics, at whatever level development is observed the same sequence appears constant across time.

Attachment is an ethological security system. Inter-subjectivity is what gives meaning to relationship and creates intimacy in both non-verbal and verbal exchanges. In the Span of Attachment, represented by the first four signs of Aries through Cancer, the child/parent relationship determines both the quality of attachment in the relationship and the capacity for inter-subjective relating. These will have enduring effects for the child in all relationships for a lifetime.

Chapter Six

The Lunar Return Model of Development: Span of Relationship and Span of the World

The next two spans of development encompass the years of seven to twenty-seven and a third years. In this astrological model it becomes clear that an attempt to accentuate the importance of only the first few years of growth is short sighted. While the initial years do set the templates for attachment and intersubjectivity in relationships, as well as many other capacities, it is the later years that determine how growth proceeds outside the home, as a result of earlier attachment history, and also how it proceeds as a result of new input from other relationships and personal goals, and involvement with community.

The Span of Relationship—Leo through Scorpio

The next four signs comprise the Span of Relationship. This span refers to the development of relationships outside the family. This span contains four stages, ruled by the signs of Leo through Scorpio, that reflect development from puberty through adolescence to early adulthood.

Leo is the first stage of development in the span of relationship. This Leo phase is approximately from seven to ten and a half years of age. Security established in the earlier attachment stages predicts a sense of confidence, competency, self-esteem, and even leadership ability in early childhood[1]. The securely attached child of the previous Cancer span will likely, in this Leo stage, be optimistic, self confident, assertive, and loving towards other children. Growth in early to middle childhood development is often evaluated in two distinct areas: 1) the child's ability to enter into peer groups and sustain good interactions with other children, and 2) the child's ability to form one special friendship. Forming this friendship is vitally important for development and, at the same time, it is also important to coordinate this friendship with being in a group[2]. So the success of the Leo stage is entwined with Aquarian dynamics. Repetitive features associated with the child's attachment history will now be apparent. In other words, in relationships with teachers and other children, the child will behave in ways that reinforce the same attachment dynamics of the early family life[3].

The stage following Leo is Virgo, from approximately ages ten and a half to thirteen, a time when puberty begins to develop. Just before puberty, there is a rise in frontal lobe activity. New physical and cognitive skills appear. The rational functions of the brain get a burst of energy and the ability to plan, execute and reason is increased. Changes in hormones and in the physical body are also experienced. In this Virgo phase there is a special need for structure and coherence and for scheduling a child's course of activity[4]. Encouraging differentiation and development of special talents is important. However, with puberty comes the Virgo tendencies to feel self-conscious, shy, and self-critical. All these can make this stage disturbing unless the positive Piscean attributes are accessed. Under Pisces' influence there is a pull to merge one's identity with others. Same sex friendships are very important at this time and can offer a needed experience of acceptance through peer identity. Merging into a group identity can provide an idealized sense of self, softening a personal self view that is critical. Less helpful Piscean tendencies, like being swept up by emotions or of losing identity to drugs and alcohol, can, if manifested, make this stage difficult. But through love and compassion (associated with the sign of Pisces), from friends and family, self-acceptance can develop and become a strength during this difficult transition time.

Libra, the sign of relationship, comes online at about age thirteen and continues through age fifteen and a half. This early stage of adolescence is very complex because now not only are same gender friendships important, but cross-gender friendships and intimate relationships are equally important[5]. The success of this period is more correlated with the earliest stage of life (the Aries stage) than with any other time of development[6]. In the Libra stage, the issues that come into focus are intimacy, trust and vulnerability. If these capacities were developed through the maternal relationship in the Aries stage, then they will be experienced more easily in the Libra phase. There is a Moon-Moon opposition during this time[7]. This represents the conflict between the need to depend upon mother and the need to separate from her. The capacity for separation is determined in the Aries stage, specifically as a result of trust and of having dependency needs met. The capacity for shared intimacy and healthy dependency—all associated with Libra—are necessary for individuation. As individuation is an Aries process, the Libra phase is dependent on the Aries phase for individuation from mother.

Scorpio, from ages fifteen and a half to eighteen (the exact demarcation of age could be a bit earlier or later) is the last stage in the span of relationship. During this phase the capacity for intimacy and vulnerability are standard measurements of the adolescent's development[8]. They indicate both the ability to remain open to experiences in relationships that threaten to reveal inner feelings, and also the ability to persist in intimate relationships despite intense and conflicting feelings[9]. Emotional turbulence and fluctuations in brain chemistry are hallmarks of this stage. The executive functions of the brain can go on strike during these years of late adolescence. The amygdala, which is the part of the brain which governs emotional responses, overtakes the more rational frontal lobes[10]. The resulting experience of emotional crisis and vulnerability to exposure of deep feelings can be difficult. Yet they can be mitigated by a history of secure attachment in relationships if, in the Taurus stage, physical comfort and emotional stability, good boundaries, and consistent and predictable responses, were present in family relationships.

The Span of the World—Sagittarius to Pisces

The last four stages comprise the Span of the World and expand development into the community and into the world. They culminate with the Pisces phase of surrender and acceptance. The duration of this last span is from age eighteen to the first lunar return at twenty-seven and a third years.

The first stage in the Span of the World is Sagittarius. From ages eighteen to twenty and a half, the need for physical and spiritual expansion and the need to be free to explore the unknown are expressions of growth at this time[11]. These needs can be realized in travel, in higher education, or in quest of a religious or spiritual discipline. These needs can also be realized in a rebellion against the morals and values of one's upbringing or in an exploration of the morals and values of other cultures. The cognitive interests, verbal skills, and creativity that were achievements of the Gemini stage may become determinants in the direction of the Sagittarius one. Here is the hero's journey. Versatility, love of travel, adaptability to different experiences, enjoyment of everything that is new—all the Gemini attributes—contribute to the world of adventure and exploration in this Sagittarius phase.

Then at about ages twenty and a half to twenty-three, the stage of Capricorn comes online. With the Capricorn emphasis, the previous urge to be free of constraints yields to a time of necessary limits and adjustment to the norms of societal rules[12]. There is more of a desire to fit in, to conform to life's requirements in order to achieve a sense of stability and security. Research shows that the maturity of the brain—specifically the frontal lobes—occurs in the early twenties. Reasoning in judgment is only now fully developed, because the frontal cortex—the seat of higher reasoning and of "executive functions"—has matured[13]. Building professional security can become a drive of this stage and is connected to the earlier experience of security and attachment in the family, represented by the sign of Cancer. Secure attachment in the formative years predicts leadership ability and success later in life. If the early home was not secure, then difficulties attaining or managing success, particularly with authority figures, could result. Also over-compensation through achievement could become a driving motivation. There can be a push-pull now between building a home away from family of origin and then going back home to the family for security. Or, if the early home life was not secure, building a foundation now in the early twenties, like getting married or buying a house, could provide the security that was missing earlier in life.

The Aquarius stage emerges at about ages twenty-three to twenty-five and a half. At this time, reaching out to the world in the form of peer groups, political groups, or community in general becomes a way of expressing oneself. Being part of a group or community provides an experience of being special and important[14]. If a sense of identity in the earlier Leo stage was based upon acceptance in the peer group, then in the Aquarian phase, assimilation into a group or community probably will go well. But if in the earlier Leo stage there was not a sense of acceptance by friends or a peer group, then there could be a sense of insecurity, loss of identity in a group and a feeling of being different or alone. To be a member of a society yet have freedom to be oneself—again the polarity with the opposite sign, Leo, is characteristic of the complexity of this Aquarian stage.

The last stage in the Span of the World is Pisces. This period, from age twenty-five and a half until the first lunar return heightens an awareness of one's own frailties and self-destructive patterns. This stage of development may require a surrender of former hopes and dreams to the reality of life's limitations.[15] This can be a time of introspection and isolation. However, feelings of loss or depression can be healed through spiritual or psychological guidance. The Virgo attributes of analysis and of self-analysis can be useful. Limitations in life can also be accepted if, in the Virgo stage, the capacity to work and to be of service were cultivated. To the degree that one was able to apply skills that were useful and productive, the vulnerability that can accompany this Pisces stage can be constructively channeled into work and service to the world.

Signs of the Zodiac and Corresponding Developmental Stages in the Lunar Return Model of Development

The following is a table of the signs of the zodiac from Aries to Pisces and their corresponding stages of maturation. It highlights key developmental terms associated with the twelve signs and twelve stages of development.

Span of Attachment	**Birth-8 Years**
Aries	*Stage of Emergence*
	Development of neuron connections, regulating affective and cognitive functioning.
	Earliest communication through right brain and mutual facial expressions.
	Attachment in the making.
Taurus	*Stage of Core Self*
	Development of sense of security and boundaries of self.
	Sensorimotor development.
	Sense of continuity of self.
Gemini	*Stage of the Verbal Self*
	Left brain communication along with right brain communication.
	Autonoesis—self-narration.
	Motor and language skills.
	Internalizing dyadic regulation.
	Mobility.
Cancer	*Completion of Span of Attachment*
	Internalization of attachment relationship.
	Emergence of the self based upon attachment history
	Quality of attachment bond differs with different family members.
	Family attachments, and quality of interdependencies.
Span of Relationships	**8-18 Years**
Leo	*Stage of Identity*
	Self Expression, self-confidence.
	Play and friendship in groups.
	Capacity for extroversion, leadership, optimism and play.
Virgo	*Stage of Competency*
	Rapid growth of orbitofrontal cortex, integrative center of emotional and higher cognitive functions of the brain.
	Development of motor and intellectual skills.
	Hormonal changes/puberty.
	Importance of boundaries in cross gender relationships.

Libra	*Stage of Relationship*
	Capacity for intimacy and vulnerability.
	Separation/Individuation revisited.
	Development of intimate relationships.
Scorpio	*Stage of Intimacy*
	Activation of limbic region of brain, center of intense emotions and sub-cortical survival defenses.
	Development of strong emotional and sexual intimacies, and interdependencies.
	Management of turbulent feelings.
Span of the World	**19-27$\frac{1}{3}$ Years**
Sagittarius	*Stage of Emancipation*
	Need for geographic or intellectual expansion.
	Freedom of expression in religious/spiritual belief systems.
	Development through higher education.
Capricorn	*Stage of Conformity*
	Maturity of brain development, full development of orbito-frontal cortex, and frontal cortex, the seat of rational thinking.
	Acceptance of societal structures and rules for success.
	Need to build for success and recognition for future security.
Aquarius	*Stage of the World*
	Allegiance to political, cultural, spiritual groups.
	Identification with groups and community.
	World ideals.
Pisces	*Stage of Surrender*
	Confronting reality.
	Revising hopes and dreams.
	Acceptance of self-limits.
	Service to the world.

As depicted above, growth follows a universal sequencing pattern that unfolds at age specific time frames, parallel to the signs of the zodiac. However, there are variations in the general schema of development and these variations are determined by the quality of relationship, environment, and conditioning. The next chapter describes the different ways development can emerge and how the secondary progressed Moon conveys the diversity.

Chapter Seven

The Zodiac: Developmental Themes for Life

The first part of the hypothesis of the lunar return theory states that the signs of the zodiac parallel twelve stages of development from birth to age twenty-seven and a third years.

The second part of the hypothesis states that the sign of the Moon, first in its birth position and then in its eleven subsequent progressed sign positions before its lunar return, conveys themes associated with these twelve stages of development from Aries to Pisces. More than any other position in the chart, the Moon is a symbol that can translate ideas about nurturing and growth into language that is consistent with astrology as well as with developmental psychology and neuroscience.

It takes twenty-seven and a third years for the Moon to complete one revolution through all twelve signs by secondary progression before reaching its lunar return. This comprises one full developmental cycle. The first cycle, from birth to the first lunar return, is the formative cycle. It is formative because it creates the template for all emotional and cognitive functioning that will follow later in life. Then the progressed Moon continues around a second and usually a third time, each time for twenty-seven and a third years. These later revolutions illustrate how development is both rooted in the first formative cycle, the template of growth, yet is ongoing as well, into adulthood and older age. The second and third revolutions reveal how development is constantly created and recreated in cyclical patterns.

As the Moon proceeds from its natal position to secondary progressions around the zodiac, it covers each sign in approximately two and a half years. Wherever the Moon at birth begins its journey, in whatever degree of whatever astrological sign, all twelve signs will eventually be represented by the time it completes its first lunar return. And because each sign represents a stage of growth, the Moon features a different theme or condition of growth through each sign placement.

There is a difference in how development proceeds in the abstract and how it proceeds in life. Stages of development from Aries through Pisces outlined in the lunar return model of development are divided into equal time spans with each sign governing a set chronological stage and each stage representing an age-specific time for development from birth to twenty-seven and a third years. But in reality, human growth is not so inflexibly structured. Many issues that are at the core of psychological development are not restricted to specific ages. They can surface at any time as a focus for maturation. And many external conditions determine how stages of development unfold in an individual's life.

Daniel Stern was the first developmental psychologist to propose, in his Interpersonal Theory, that many themes central to psychological development are not stage- or age-specific.[1] Examples of these are the need for autonomy, security, and intimacy. These needs emerge in the earliest years of life and continue to develop from there on. They, as well as many other needs, remain issues for the lifetime and are not limited in importance, as earlier stage theories proposed, to one specific time frame only. It is this characteristic of development, that vital themes are not limited to one stage only, that is expressed by the sign of the progressed Moon.

In addition, according to recent findings in developmental psychology, although stages may be predetermined genetically, *conditions that affect how the stages unfold are not predetermined genetically.* "Developmental research reveals that certain genetically programmed innate biological structural systems that support adaptive functioning require particular early developmental environmental input to be manifest."[2]

This does not mean that developmental psychology disregards the natural preprogramming of bio-genetic development. There is universal consensus that the genetic code still bears the indelible marks of evolution[3] and that biological stages do unfold in timed sequences. The lunar return model mirrors the nature of this course. But every stage of growth requires relational or environmental participation in order to be fulfilled.[4] The quality of every stage is determined by the impact of living relationships and environmental conditions. And it is this variability of conditions that is conveyed through the sign of the Moon.

A natal Moon in any one of thirty degrees in any one of twelve signs will initiate a unique unfolding of a twelve stage developmental sequence. Each sign of the progressed Moon signs will determine the themes and conditions that determine how nature's stages manifest. Therefore, any interpretation of development through the sign of the Moon requires the awareness that something essential about development is unique for each person.

If a progressed Moon is in Aries, a challenge to individuation arises regardless of the age of the person. The natural, biological, Aries stage occurs from birth to age two and a half. But a sense of autonomy, symbolized by the sign of Aries, takes years to develop and is likely to gain strength later in the child's developing years. A progressed Moon in Aries for a sixteen-year-old could describe just this process. Age sixteen is a stage when teenagers begin to form more intimate relationships than they had in earlier adolescence. Perhaps the Moon in Aries at this age could occur at a time when an intimate relationship supports the development of autonomy. At sixteen the need to assert autonomy by separating from one's relationships with family or friends is stronger than at any preceding age. The Aries Moon might describe a conflict between the need to explore intimate relationships and a condition that prevents it, that creates aloneness or separation, and thereby encourages autonomy by default.

A progressed Moon in Taurus at age two would coincide chronologically with the second phase of development that governs the surfacing of a core sense of self, the self that recognizes its body, its form, and a sense of continuity over time. A progressed Moon in Taurus at age sixteen, however, would encounter some challenge of Taurus development at an age and stage of growth well beyond the toddler years when Taurus development naturally unfolds. The progressed Moon in Taurus at age sixteen does not mean that development that should have occurred at age two was completely arrested and is taking place instead at age sixteen. Instead it could mean that some expression or need associated with Taurus development is calling for attention at age sixteen. It could express itself as the need for safety and continuity in relationships. And even though sixteen is an age when many adolescents would need more risk and experiment in their activities and with members of the opposite sex, there is no set norm. The point is that the Taurus sense of self is making its appearance at a time that is necessary for this individual at sixteen in alignment with this individual's unique course of development.

If a client who is 19 has his progressed Moon in Taurus, some element of the second phase of development—perhaps the need for tangible security—is applicable to the nineteen-year-old, even though he is in a phase symbolically represented in our abstract timetable of development by the sign of Sagittarius, which signifies a time of breaking free, rebelling, taking risks to express one's freedom. Instead, with the Moon in Taurus, perhaps a stronger desire for security at this time dominates this individual's life and achieving that would be the important developmental task at this time. So the 19-year-old, according to a generic map of growth, should be in a time of expansion but the Taurus Moon shows how development is modified by the goals or conditions associated with the sign of Taurus.

Another example is the progressed Moon in Cancer. Even though every child forms an attachment bond by age seven or eight months, for a child whose progressed Moon reaches Cancer at age six, attachment issues might be crucial to the developing character of the individual at this time. And so from six years of age through the next two and a half years that progressed Moon in Cancer will set the stage for the attachment that will likely exert influence on relationships for an entire lifetime.

The house position of the progressed Moon provides a context for understanding how or where a process is being experienced. Houses, in this sense, are the environments in which an individual's experience is formed. If the Moon moves into the first house, it has meaning in an Aries context and describes identification with something that is beginning, something that is new. The Moon crossing into the first house in the sign of Virgo could signal the beginning of a health regimen or a job. If the Moon moves into Capricorn in the fifth house, insecurity and shyness may be overcome through artistic expression.

The progressed Moon's aspects to other planets defines how its expression is limited, enhanced or affected by the qualities of those other planets. A progressed Moon in Sagittarius might initiate a period of freedom for exploration or self-expression, or a time of a quest for one's truth, spiritually or emotionally. But if this Moon forms a T-square, for example, to a Venus-Pluto conjunction in Virgo, and another square to Saturn in Pisces, this phase might feel like a complete upheaval. So here the freedom of the Moon may not be indicative of an inspiring experience of adventure, but rather an experience that cuts right to the heart and challenges the individual to find steady ground when life feels like a roller coaster.

The Moon sign, therefore, in the lunar return model of development is interpreted either in terms of central themes of psycho-social development or in terms of an interweaving of predetermined stages of development and relational dynamics that activate these stages and create a relational sense of self. According to Interpersonal Theory in developmental psychology, a child gains a sense of self in the intersubjective relationship with mother during the first eighteen months of life. Senses of self that are born in the inter-subjective space of relationship are interwoven with biological and neurological time lines of developmental stages because, it turns out, they are reciprocally and mutually dependent. For example, the mother's attunement to her infant creates neurotransmitters in the brain of her child that are responsible for regulating stress.[5] The child who can regulate stress, can also self-sooth and will be able to psychologically separate from the mother without emotional trauma at the times that are biological and genetically coded for separation processes.

Therefore, the Aries self, the emergent self, is a result of relational interactions between mother and child during the Aries stage of development. And the same with the Taurus core self, the Gemini verbal self, the Cancer intersubjective self, and so on through Pisces, with all twelve signs representing different parts of a whole self that result from the transactional dynamics in relationships during maturational stages. Therefore, when we look at how the signs of the zodiac correspond with psychological development, it is possible to see signs correlate with both a stepwise timeline of development and with domains of self-development that are expressions of the richness and variation of communication that occur in states of relational interdependency.

In the lunar return model, development, under each sign's dominance, continues, even after each sign has come online. Instead of tapering off its influence after it has been in the limelight of development, a feature of maturation continues to develop. Once a theme of development has been awakened, it will continue on its evolutionary path for a lifetime.

The lunar return model of development is also multi-layered; twelve aspects of self can evolve simultaneously once they have all emerged.[6] One does not supplant another as the progressed Moon moves through the sequence of signs in the zodiac. The Aries emergent self—the capacity to initiate engagement in relationship with another—does not go away when the Taurus core self comes online. The Taurus sense of self does not diminish when the Gemini, the verbal self, is dominant. The Gemini phase of development in our astrological model occurs between ages three and a half and five and focuses on the dual modes of thinking—right- and left-brain—that happen to connect most actively at this time. But before age three and a half, children are very actively communicating in relationships. And after age five the verbal self is clearly still active. So the domain of the verbal self, described within the Gemini stage between ages three and a half and five, actually exists in some form before age four and continues after age six for the entire lifetime. The stage of Cancer from ages five through six in the lunar model of development states that attachment patterns are firmly established within the family system during this phase. But the theme of attachment under the sign of Cancer can easily emerge as a dominant life issue at any time prior or after age eight as well. Attachment is a theme for life.

Many of the examples in this chapter have referred to stages of growth during the first lunar cycle from birth to twenty-seven and a third years, when the sign of the Moon reflects early development. The next chapters will further illustrate case examples of the progressed Moon, both in the formative cycle, as well as in following cycles in which development is reiterative and progressive at the same time.

Chapter Eight

Rotations and Revelations of the Secondary Progressed Moon

Chaos theory[1] states that every system in the universe moves toward greater and greater complexity and is always being stabilized by forces of chaos and order. Developmental processes mirrored through the progressed Moon reflect these very interactions of randomness and order in nature. In the symbolic world of astrology, the Moon represents the feeding of external input into the astrology chart itself, igniting internal structures of the chart with new aspects and aspect patterns that assemble and reassemble as the Moon moves in and out of orb with other planets. The internal structures and representations in the birth chart have order but they are open to new interpretations that are catalyzed by the Moon—the external information bearer.

In this way the progressed Moon activates the inherent potential of the birth chart, or current potential of the progressed chart. If a client has the progressed Moon in Leo conjunct natal Pluto, natal Pluto is the pre-set internal structure, and the Moon is the channel from the outside world that flows into the chart, the symbol for the spontaneous counterpart of development. The sign of the Moon in Leo represents the developmental issue that has come on-line. The progressed Moon in Leo poses a developmental challenge to one's sense of self value, of importance, which is often derived from a love relationship. As life brings in circumstances that allow one's value to be realized, the contact with Pluto may temporarily destroy a source of love or recognition in order to supply another basis for self value. The Moon in Leo might then introduce a new relational experience, that could replace the old and alter one's sense of value or capacity to love.

The astrology chart is ordered in nature by the patterns governing it at birth, but it is permeable as well. All systems that grow—and here the astrology chart is a system—must always be open to new information from the outside. All systems that are open to new information become more complex and thereby achieve greater stability than systems that remain closed to new information. A closed system that does not allow new information will die. The challenge to accommodate and adapt to high levels of complexity must be met with permeability. The progressed Moon addresses this function.

Within the definition of chaos theory, outcomes are always open to laws of spontaneity and randomness that govern complex systems. And progressions in the astrology chart are subject to these same laws. The exact effects on the individual's experience of even the most accurately timed progression cannot be planned. One can speculate about the outcome of a symbol and placement of any astrological configuration, but the exact experience that will shape meaning and direction of life is unpredictable—until it happens. What will give the chart meaning is the actual experience in life that results. Then the real meaning of experience can be integrated into the interpretation of the entire chart. Before then, every possible manifestation of a symbol hovers in a state of virtual reality.

The Moon, more than any other planet, makes the interdependency between order and disorder visible because its movements are always changing, adding and receiving new information that shapes and reshapes patterns in the chart. The Moon is the catalyst for the rest of the chart, igniting the energy of planets it illuminates. In *The Eagle and the Lark*, Bernadette Brady reveals that in ancient times the Moon was called "translator of light," a carrier of energy from one planet to another.[2] The progressed Moon's sign, she states, reflects the kind of energy one is seeking—"the type of experiences toward which you will unconsciously gravitate"—and is a catalyst for the planets and planetary patterns in the birth chart. It highlights and carries energy from one part of the chart to another. It triggers the energy inherent in the chart and in this way has its own unique function.

The astrology chart looks static. But the chart is really a dynamic system and, like the internal world of the individual, the system is constantly poised between upheaval and stability. The Moon's play on the astrology chart is the abstract rendition of the ongoing process of energy exchanges between the internal world of the self and the external world of the environment that defines and redefines relational growth.

The example charts in this chapter are intended to illustrate how the secondary progressed Moon, during the first twenty-seven and a third years of life, captures a unique picture in time of an individual's developmental path. The first three examples are the charts of children whose experiences were communicated through the perception of their mothers. In all other chart examples the meaning attributed to the progressed Moon is based upon client self-report. The reader can discern the importance of other placements in the chart, but the focus here is on the client's subjective experience, expressed in his or her own words, and reflected by the progressed Moon.

Interpretations for the progressed Moon vary for each client even though it may be in the same sign for two people. However, in these cases the interpretations speak to the same area of development pertinent to that sign. In addition, any meaning attributed to the Moon needs to be integrated with the rest of the chart. In interpreting any astrology chart, the important themes will be repeated by a number of signatures in the chart, and the progressed Moon will usually be among them.

The examples on the following pages, including charts and descriptions, are from the author's files.

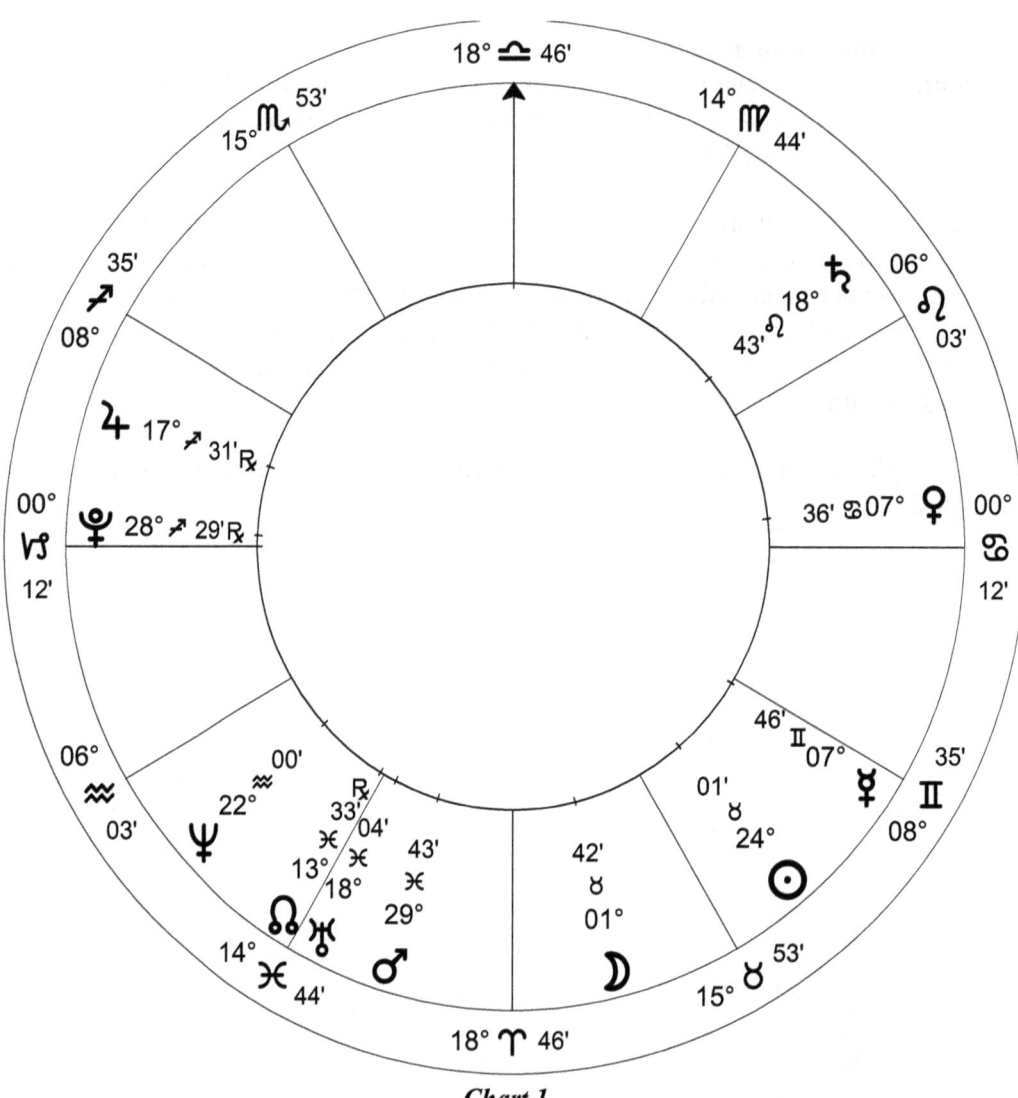

Chart 1.
May 14, 2007, 10:32 p.m. PDT, Glendale, California

In Chart 1 the natal Moon is in Taurus in the fourth house. This is the chart of a seven-month-old girl, born into a stable home environment with loving parents and many family members who are emotionally and financially involved in her well-being. Favorable alignments to other planets, including Venus in Cancer, support the interpretation of this child's need for and ability to gain the love of her family. In addition, her mother reports that her baby is very expressive, especially physically. The significance of the Taurus placement at birth suggests that a mutual communication system between mother and child that from the very onset of life promotes strong physicality and emotional stability.

58/The Progressed Moon Around the Zodiac

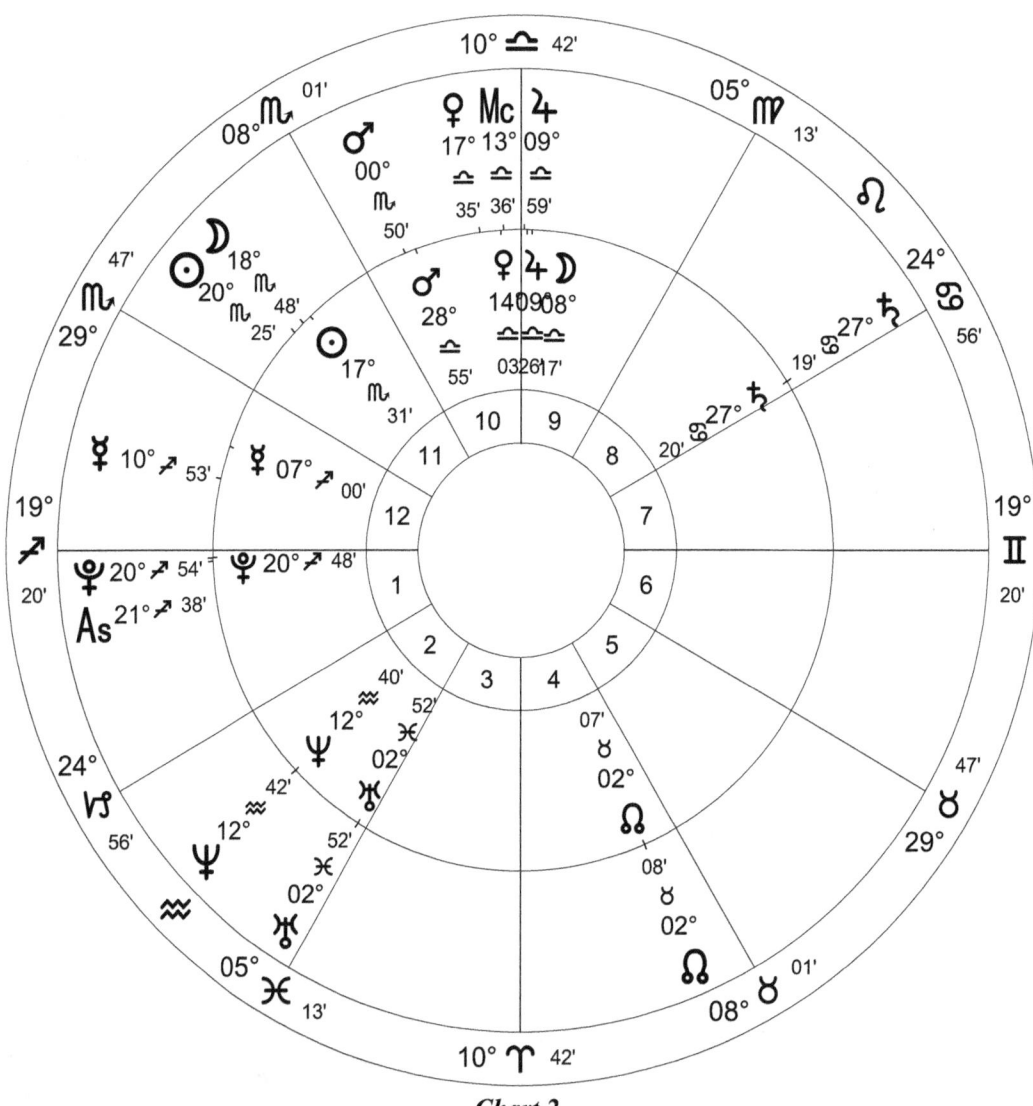

Chart 2.
Inner Wheel: Natal, November 9, 2004, 9:19 a.m. EST, New York, New York.
Outer Wheel: Progressed

Chart 2 is the chart of two-year-old fraternal twins. Their progressed Moons are in the sign of Scorpio in the eleventh house. These two babies were famous from the moment of their birth their mother conceived them at age fifty-six, usually beyond the childbearing years. Now these two children have a strong and loving mother who is single and must work hard to support them. They also have an extended family of mother's friends who all contribute to their well-being. The twins have developed emotional attachments to these benefactors. During their Taurus stage of development, they appear to derive emotional security from this loving group. Their interdependency with each other as well as with the group, describe the Scorpio influence on their development. And in the eleventh house, they are truly children of the world.

60/The Progressed Moon Around the Zodiac

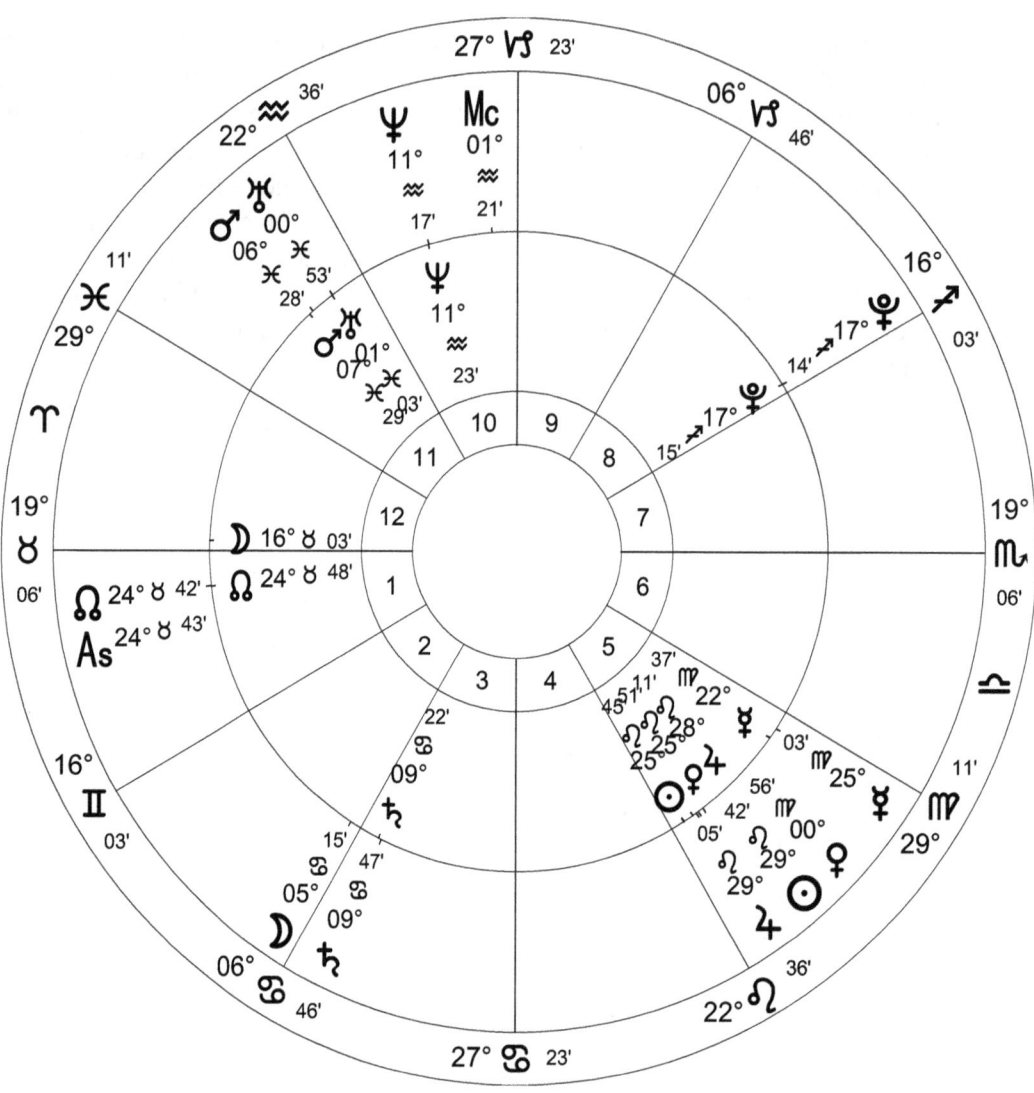

Chart 3.
Inner Wheel: Natal, August 18, 2003, 11:20 p.m., Rochester, New York
Outer Wheel: Progressed

Chart 3 is the chart of a child of six whose progressed Moon in Cancer symbolizes the attachment issues that prevail in his life. His parents are threatening divorce, and the climate is controlling and hostile. His mother expresses some desire to take her son away from her husband who she fears because he has behaved violently and irrationally toward her. The progressed Moon in Cancer describes this child's protective feelings for his mother. With the Moon approaching natal Saturn in Cancer, it is possible that his mother's separation from his father and family members will produce anxiety in this child, and no doubt become a crucial theme in his attachment history. Attachment in the family is represented by stage four in the lunar return model (ages seven and a half through nine). But, again, even though the fourth stage ideally represents attachment themes in the family, attachment issues are for the lifetime and not relegated to one stage only.

62/The Progressed Moon Around the Zodiac

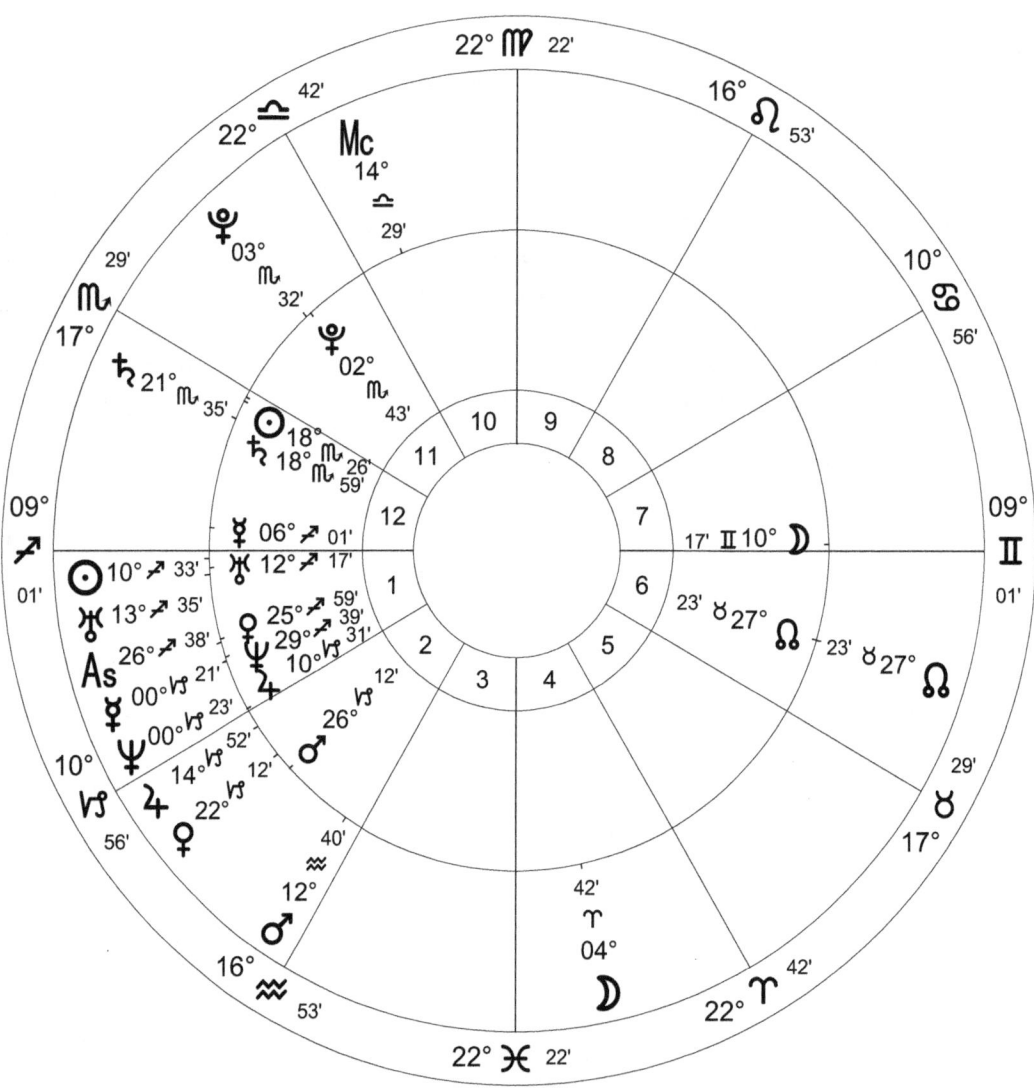

Chart 4.
Inner Wheel: Natal, November 10, 1984, 8:05 a.m. PST, Los Angeles
Outer Wheel: Progressed

Chart 4 is the chart of a woman who at the time of her reading was age twenty-one, with the progressed Moon in Aries in the fourth house. At twenty-one, the natural stage of Capricorn reflected her need to find an identity in the world upon which to build her future. This woman had a very clear sense of herself and a sense of independence beyond her years. This independence had been encouraged by her parents her entire life and, therefore, at age twenty-one she was eager to travel and to pursue her interests abroad. Although she had this sense of adventure, she still experienced separation anxiety from her family.

The progressed Moon in Aries in the fourth house, natural house of Cancer, symbolizes a transitional phase in this woman's life in which she felt conflicted between wanting to explore her independence and wanting to remain at home. Resolute and very enthusiastic to begin her new life, the desire for self-exploration was eventually stronger than any need for family or relationships. So here the progressed Moon in Aries expresses the sense of initiative that had been nurtured by her parents, as well as the internal conflict she experienced for a while about further separation from her family.

64/The Progressed Moon Around the Zodiac

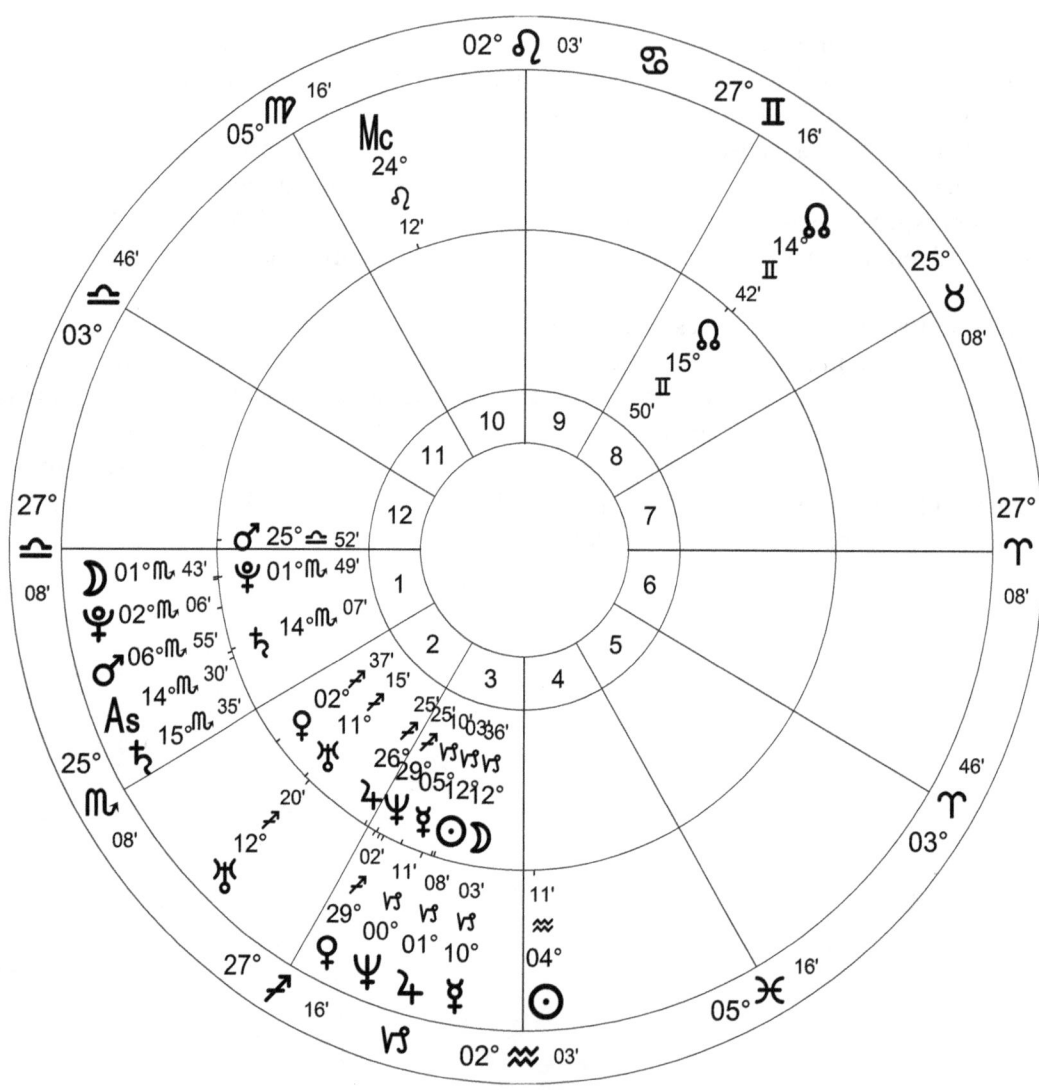

Chart 5.
Inner Wheel: Natal, January 3, 1983, 1:25 a.m. EST, New York, New York
Outer Wheel: Progressed

Chart 5 is that of a woman, age twenty-two, who had her progressed Moon in Scorpio in the first house. Although this woman was in a Capricorn stage of development, one in which building a sense of self in the external world depends upon an internal state of security, she was not feeling secure internally. She had always experienced intense dependency needs on her mother. Now, at age twenty-two, these needs were transferred onto anyone with whom she became emotionally involved, at the level of friendship or romance.

There had been a history earlier in her life of relationships blowing up and ending because she would come on so strong with her emotional needs that she distanced people. Her natal Mars conjunct Pluto reflects the intensity of her possessiveness and need to control others because of these dependency needs. With the progressed Moon in Scorpio, she was truly trying to master her intense emotions and trying to become aware of the unconscious ways she was expressing desires in relationships.

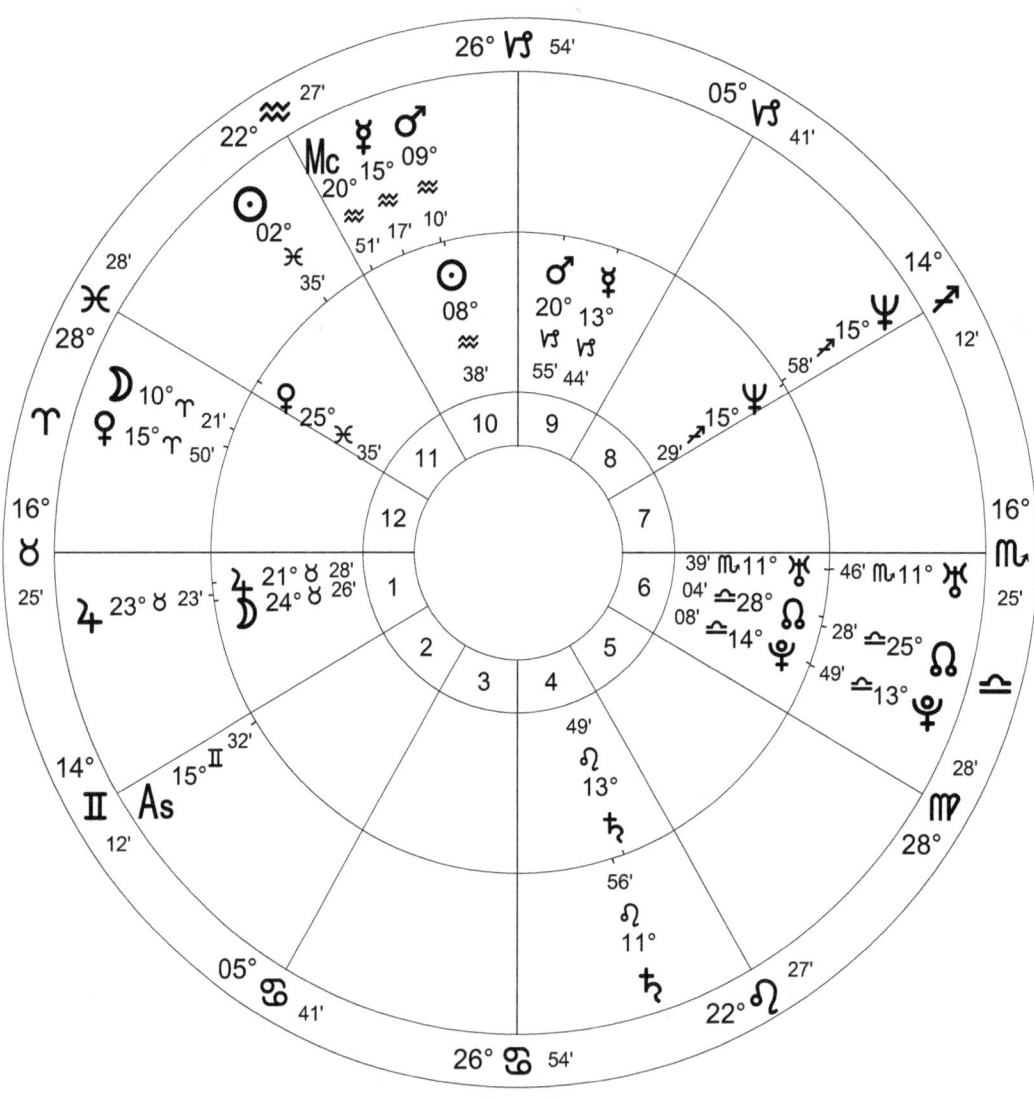

Chart 6.
Inner Wheel: Natal, January 28, 1977, 11:20 a.m. EST, Queens, New York
Outer Wheel: Progressed

Chart 6 is another example of the progressed Moon in Aries in the twelfth house. This client was age twenty-three at the time of his reading and was experiencing an identity crisis, a real sense of loss of self. He was depressed because he felt that he had no strong sense of himself or of his individuality. He felt he had so adapted himself to please others that he did not even know who he was. So even though he was twenty-three, he was struggling with the developmental issues of the sign of Aries in order to acquire a clearer sense of his autonomy and an ability to assertively change his world.

68/The Progressed Moon Around the Zodiac

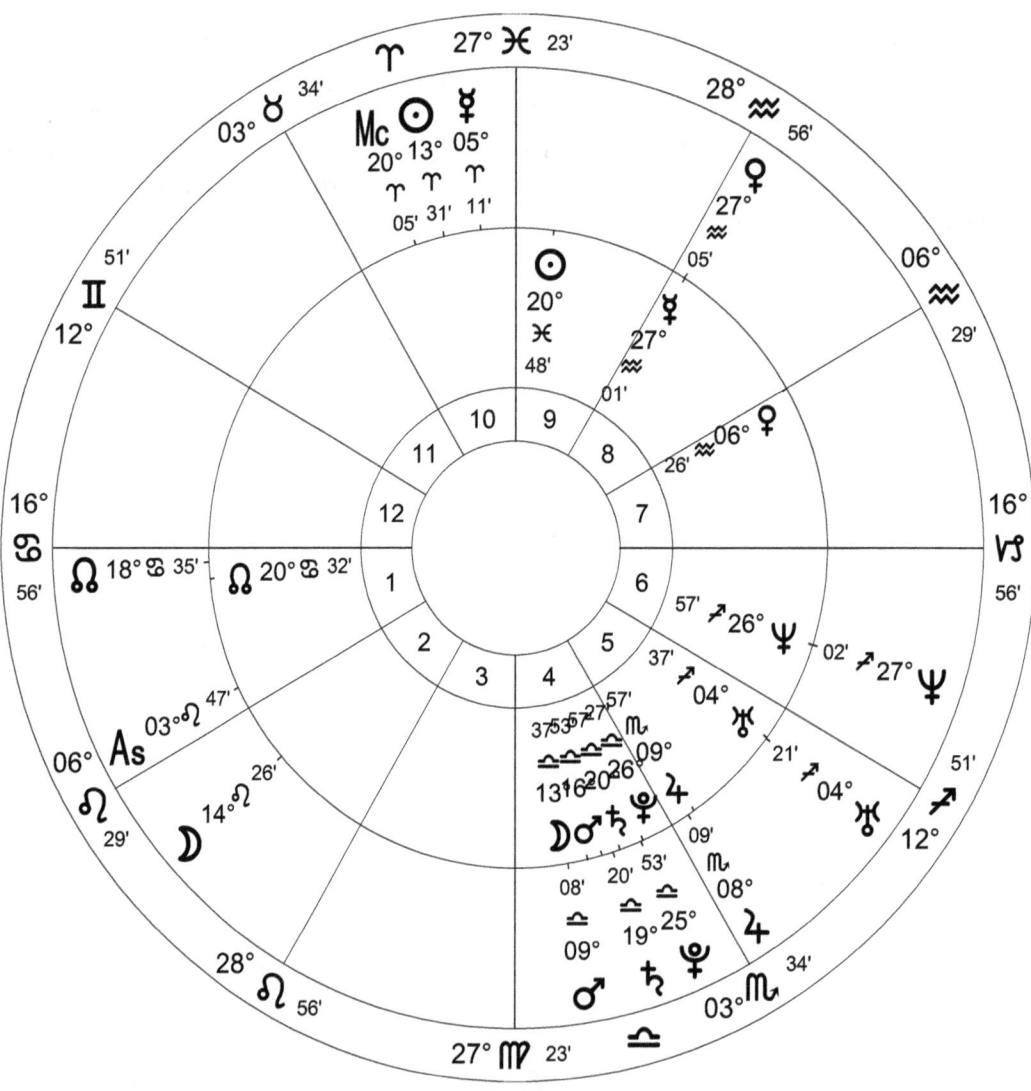

Chart 7.
Inner Wheel: Natal, March 11, 1982, 12:30 p.m. EST, Long Island City, New York
Outer Wheel: Progressed

Chart 7 is a twenty-four-year-old woman who was working as a waitress when her progrssed Moon was in Leo. She was underpaid and under-valued at this job. She had a boyfriend but it was not clear that she felt loved or special to him. She did not feel appreciated by her family, whose needs she had prioritized for many years. Although she felt she had lost all sense of personal direction, the progressed Moon's cycle through Leo helped her decide to go back to school to pursue a career in education working with children.

So at age twenty-four, the natural age for the Aquarius phase in which group identification is sought, this individual needed to develop a sense of her own value and had to separate from group identifications. This is the symmetrical opposite of the need of the Aquarius stage of life, or of a typical interpretation of this stage. Instead, this young woman needed to separate her identity from her group involvements at her job and in her family and seek to define her own special abilities apart from them.

70/The Progressed Moon Around the Zodiac

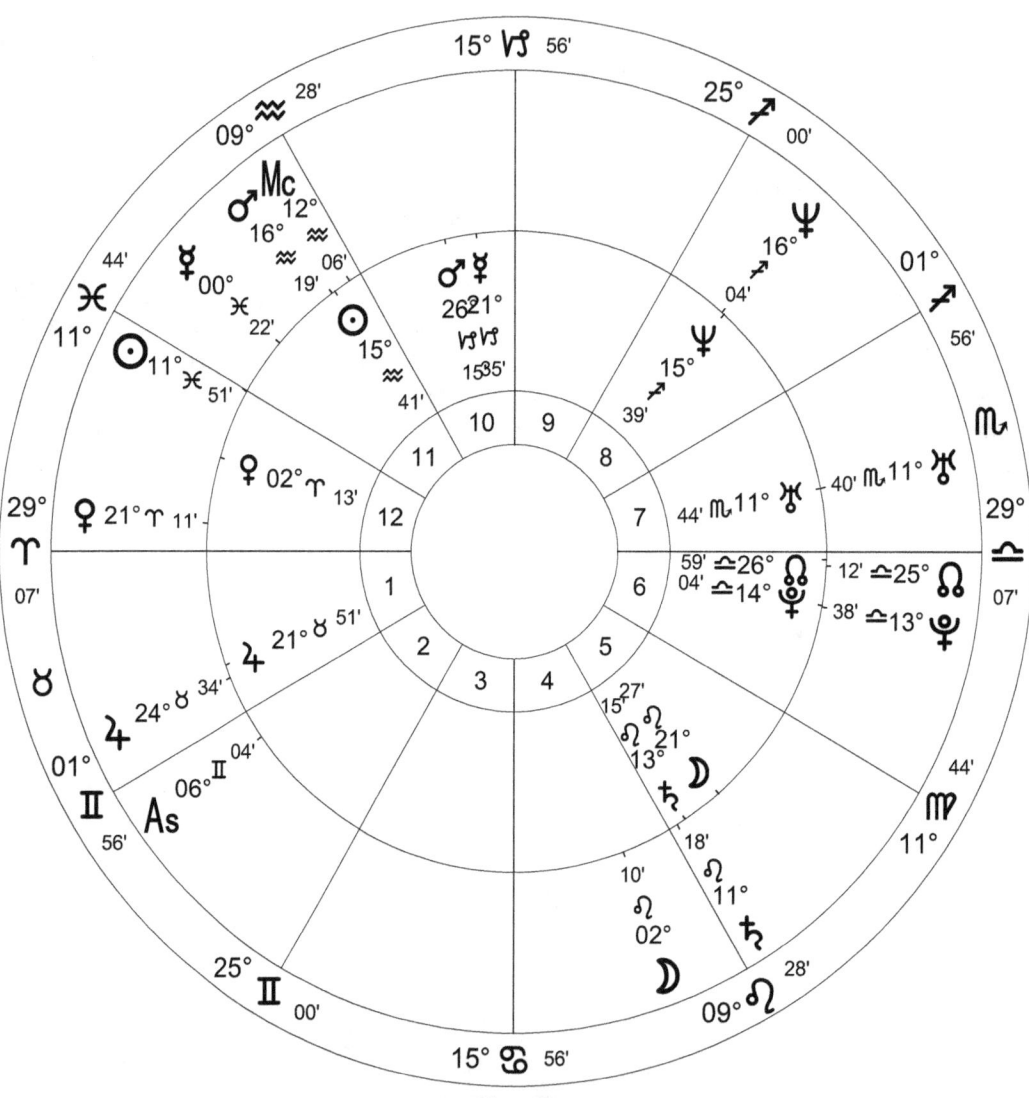

Chart 8.
Inner Wheel: Natal, February 4, 1977, 10:06 a.m. EST, Queens, New York
Outer Wheel: Progressed

Chart 8 is the chart of a twenty-five-year-old man whose progressed Moon in Leo was in the fourth house. He was struggling with his family over lifelong issues of not feeling appreciated by them. The youngest in a family of five siblings, he felt infantilized by them, and although he was talented musically, his ability was not taken seriously. He was both financially dependent upon family and hurt by their doubts about his future. The developmental challenge of a progressed Moon in Leo is to build self-confidence and to find a source of feeling special and valued. Because this person's natal Moon was conjunct Saturn in his fifth house, self-doubt and self-consciousness were vulnerabilities from birth and accentuated the importance of this progressed Moon stage.

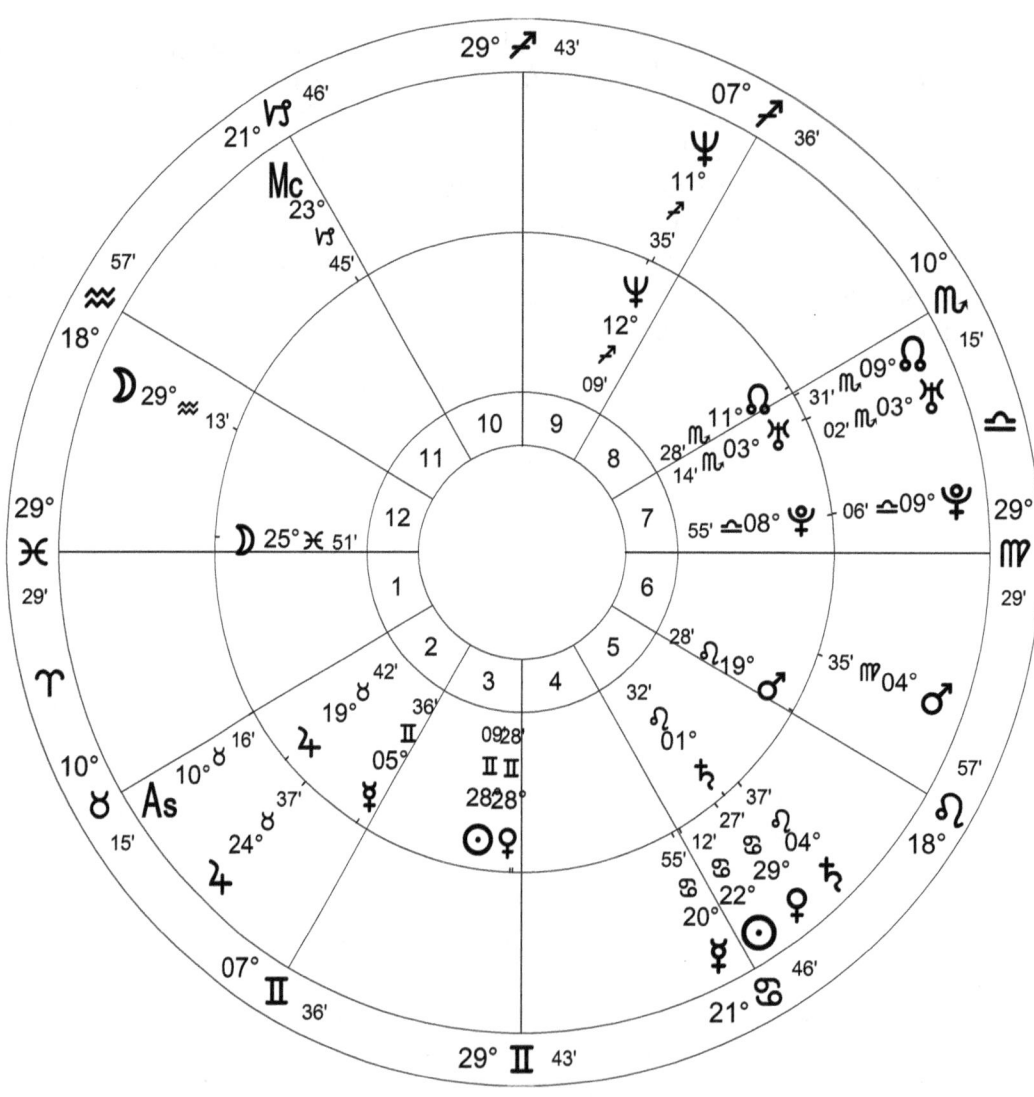

Chart 9.
Inner Wheel: Natal, June 19, 1976, 1:15 a.m. PDT, Davis, California
Outer Wheel: Progressed

Chart 9 is the last example of the developmental influence of the progressed Moon in its first cycle. The client was age twenty-six and a half when her progressed Moon entered the sign of Aquarius. Because her natal Moon is in Pisces, her progressed Moon in Aquarius was one developmental stage before her first lunar return. The sign that appears before a lunar return conveys its own characteristic themes but here with a Piscean twist because it is the twelfth stage, the last before the Moon finalizes its journey around the chart. In this woman's case, she had believed in the good-heartedness of a friend who instead betrayed her, both professionally and personally. Not only did she experience this disappointment, but there were other friends as well who let her down during this time. She lost trust in her judgment of people and felt that her only recourse was to disengage from them.

As it progresses from birth through the sequence of signs in the zodiac, the Moon operates as a relational system and mirrors development that is co-created between self and others. The others are family members, friends, romantic relationships and all external circumstances that mold and change internal experiences. The sign of the Moon signifies the specific issues and themes of development that arise in the ongoing process of maturation. When the Moon appears in its second and third cycles in the same signs and in the same angular relationships to planets in the birth chart that it occupeid in the natal chart, its repetitions can afford each person an opportunity to cope with and respond differently to the issues that are awakened under its influence.

Meanings of Progressed Moon in 12 Signs Correlating to Developmental Themes

Moon in Aries	Emergence	Beginning something new. Being on one's own. Being alone or individuated.
Moon in Taurus	Security	Establishing stability. Need for solidity and strength. Having resources that other people want or need.
Moon in Gemini	Communication	Needing skills in communication. Bifurcation of experience. Learning new skills. Focus on twinship or sibling relations.
Moon in Cancer	Attachment	Replication of attachment in a current relationship. Attachment needs expressed as addictions. Mother in one's life. Need to nurture or self-nurture.
Moon in Leo	Identity	Need to feel valued through love, art, or children. Capacity for play or self expression. Need to feel recognition.
Moon in Virgo	Mastery	Development of skills. Choice of work. Health concerns. Need to establish healthy routines.
Moon in Libra	Partnership	Need for a partner. Partnership challenge. Meeting a partner. Partnership opportunities. Dependency in relationships.
Moon in Scorpio	Dependency	Interdependencies, financial, emotional, or sexual. Endings, clearing out the old. Ventures with other people and their money.
Moon in Sagittarius	Expansion	Risk, venture, travel. Teaching, publication. Urgency, speed, stress. Courting danger. Freedom without anchor.

Moon in Capricorn	Limits	Need to be organized.
		Need to tolerate structure.
		Conformity, restrictions, or sense of limits.
		Fear of rejection.
Moon in Aquarius	Freedom	Freedom or distancing.
		Need to try something new.
		Friendship and quality of friendship.
		Group involvement
		Eccentric or irrational people.
Moon in Pisces	Surrender	Need to let go, go with the flow.
		Sense of sorrow or loss.
		Isolation.
		Service to others.
		Illness and healing.

The secondary progressed Moon in its cycles around the zodiac is a specific indicator of emotional and spiritual growth. In Brian Clark's article, "The Progressed Moon: Mnemosye's Recollections,"[3] he states: "The secondary progressed Moon is the most appropriate astrological calendar for recording the emotional maturation and evolution of the individual." The progressed Moon, in its sign and house placement and aspect patterns, provides an access route for understanding a core developmental process. This access route has immediacy; it reflects the internal experience of a condition or challenge in life. It represents the emotional world of the client as it is co-created in the immediacy of living experience.

Chapter Nine

Repetitive Themes on the
Circular Pathway of Development

"The progressed Moon symbolizes our continuous search to belong, to remember, to renew. It is also a continuous cycle of loss and recovery of our emotional attachments."[1]

The third part of the hypothesis of the lunar return model of development is that the pathway of human growth is not linear, as it is in traditional psychology, but circular, as the progressed Moon travels around the horoscope up to three times in a lifespan. Birth to age twenty-seven and four months constitutes the first cycle, age twenty-seven and four months to fifty-four and eight months is the second cycle, and then, from age fifty and eight months to eighty-two years is the third cycle. Some will live longer to experience part of a fourth cycle as well. The first twenty-seven years provide the earliest and formative experiences of growth while the following cycles provide more mature versions, as well as opportunities to better resolve difficulties that arise in the formative years of life. Developmental challenges that arise during the first and formative cycle of growth—birth to the first lunar return—can reappear in patterns of behavioral or emotional responses in the second and even third cycles when the progressed Moon contacts the same natal positions it occupied during the formative stages of development. Similar experiences are likely to occur that can offer opportunity for change. These similar experiences can be cloaked in different garb from one cycle to another, but something essential about the developmental theme will be the same.

This repetition phenomenon is akin to Rupert Sheldrake's biomorphic field theory[4]. This theory explains continuity over time, how everything goes on being, based upon the nature of fields. In Rupert Sheldrake's model, everything in the universe, whether a crystal or a bird or a tree or even an abstract body, like a government or society, has a field of energy that changes and develops through its own habits and customs. Fields that comprise all the characteristics and structures of the crystal, or bird, or tree, or body of government continue because they have "self-resonance." This means that fields of energy are sustained and can continue to go on through time because they have memory of their own past states of being. Memory is equivalent to resonance. Rituals are an example of this resonance. When a ritual is performed and has meaning, it comes to life not because of the external motions of the ritual but because it has memory of its past. And it is this remembrance that echoes through time and provides continuity.

In a similar way, the fields of the progressed Moon hold memory and self-resonance. As it rotates around the chart, the progressed Moon re-contacts the same angles and the same planets as it did in a former cycle and the same developmental themes can be awakened by memories of the past.

The term "developmental" in the lunar return model refers to growth that is both experience/relational dependent as well as age dependent. Many psychologists, including Erik Erikson and Carl Jung, based significant parts of their careers on observable transitions in adult development. In *Passages* Gail Sheehy delineates the stages that are characteristic of adulthood from age thirty through sixty. The lunar return model also extends development from youth into adulthood and older age, but, as with the first cycle of growth, development is not just linear along the axis of age, but circular. The same twelve signs always circle around, reflecting their developmental meaning through the position of the progressed Moon. Social, intellectual, and spiritual development unfolds in the context of evolving maturation according to each individual's age and experience.

The term "developmental" can also apply to the challenge that one must undertake in order to master tasks of complexity associated with a specific stage of life. In the first cycle this could apply to language development, math, and reasoning skills, and social development. In the second cycle, mastery could refer to professional or educational pursuits, or even to the ability to balance responsibilities to family and career simultaneously. All developmental achievements in any cycle are measurements of many factors, including inherent ability and the impact of the environment. However, there is a dyadic component of development regardless of which cycle the progressed Moon is traversing. Dr. Daniel Siegel of the Department of Psychiatry at UCLA has proposed that supportive relationships can positively affect brain chemistry well into adulthood.[2] In addition, studies affirm that psychotherapy helps clients regulate mood and stress levels, and this can be shown in brain scan imaging. The capacity of a client to improve in relational psychotherapy becomes evident in his or her ability to self reflect, self soothe, access emotional states, verbalize feelings, and enter into relatively healthy relationships that were not possible prior to treatment. These resulting improvements can again be measured with brain chemistry techniques. Extrapolating from these studies, researchers conclude that enduring effects of all supportive and empathic relationships in adulthood can increase neuron activity and alter brain functioning.

The term "developmental" can also refer to one's ability to accept and often overcome the unexpected difficulties that life presents, and to mature as a result. In this scenario life imposes its own will—through illness, birth, death, and even sudden and unexpected opportunities. This kind of development can occur during any and all cycles of the progressed Moon.

Regardless of a person's age, the themes associated with a sign of the progressed Moon will be the same in all cycles. And every category of growth has its own maturation process. For example, in the first cycle, between the ages of three and a half to five, Gemini represents the focus of growth, and the emphasis is on language development, play, and early social development. During the second and third cycles, maturation along the Gemini line of growth will continue to involve learning, communicating, and self-expression but in ways that reflect the biological and psychological maturation process of an older adult. In the second cycle, mastery in the Gemini area of growth could apply to the ability to think and reason on several levels—practical, ethical, and intuitive—in order to function as a mature person in society. And during the third cycle this Gemini category of maturation can refer to the way learning, perception and cognitive processes are influenced by age and personal experience.

Every sign has its own maturation process that begins in the formative cycle of life. In the second and third cycles, the meanings of each sign reflect both the biological and psychological growth process and the specific ways the generic and specific blend for each person. Aries in the formative cycle represents the capacity for individuation, built upon a secure attachment within a primary relationship. Aries in midlife can refer to the capacity for self-initiative, for leadership ability, for courage in facing life's challenges. And Aries in later years might relate to one's capacity to be alone, to begin all over again in new relationships, and in new endeavors that are consistent with one's age and life transitions.

As it progresses in time, sign, and cycle, the progressed Moon continues to function as a self-other configuration, meaning it represents both oneself and the influence of another. Of course, this can be another person in the individual's life, but the other can also refer to an event or involvement that triggers memory of significant others and has enriching capacity as well as personal meaning. The study of self psychology explains how music, film, or learning a new skill can fulfill "self-object functions"[3] in adulthood. A self-object function refers to an individual's involvement with a person or activity that enhances that individual's sense of self. So, the original self-object is mother in that the mother affirms the child's being. Later in life, a self-object can be interests and activities that are reminders of these earlier affirmations of talents and strengths received in the relationship with an acknowledging mother or caregiver. A progressed Moon in Libra in the fifth house, for example, in a second or third lunar cycle, might manifest as development of talent and taste in music or design which at an earlier age might have originated in relationship with a mother who actively encouraged her daughter's learning of music and design, or who participated with her in these activities. Development is still relational but here the relationship is to beauty and art.

The direction of growth for each person's Moon sign depends upon the unique factors of that person's life, in particular on the earliest attachment experiences. If an individual with a natal Moon in Aries had a good enough attachment relationship in childhood, then a progressed Moon in Aries later on is likely to feel empowering. This person would be able to initiate a new direction in life without fear of being alone.

A Libra Moon in the first cycle might reflect the ability to establish intimacy in relationships and, if this was successfully achieved, then in the second cycle the Libra Moon might indicate a good marriage or manifest as a partnership in business or artistic ventures. The ability to enter into partnership is based upon a mature balance between the need for dependency and the need for autonomy. In the third cycle of the Libra Moon the individual may be able to accept more dependency on another person and rely upon interpersonal skills to draw on social support systems that are important for maintaining physical health and emotional well being.

Often there will be an opportunity, in the second or third cycle of the progressed Moon, to respond more effectively and productively to situations that were difficult earlier in life. It is not that a literal event repeats in the second or third cycle, but its meaning repeats at important junctures in subsequent cycles. These junctures can occur when the Moon crosses an axis point, or enters a new house, or makes an aspect to the same natal planet it contacted in its first and formative cycle.

While signs are emphasized in this Lunar Model of Growth, aspects to the natal Moon are also important. A natal Moon opposing natal Uranus may describe an anxious attachment, one in which a child feels insecure in relationship to his mother. Mother may detach or have unpredictable mood swings. When the progressed Moon revisits this natal opposition, it can awaken a compulsion to break a bond, or it can be experienced as an unwanted disconnection from an important attachment relationship. The individual may feel compelled to break a bond, or experience an unwanted disconnection from an important attachment relationship. Later, in the third cycle, an individual whose progressed Moon contacts this natal Moon Uranus opposition, may come to understand that he or she has conflicting needs, one part needing attachment and intimacy, the other fearing commitment, being trapped, or abandoned. Being aware that these two sides of oneself are in conflict may prevent compulsive acting out and enhance the ability to choose healthy relationships.

The progressed Moon is in each sign for two and a half years. There are many ways a person can learn to respond differently to certain kinds of experiences that present over and over again during this period of time. What constitutes a mending of the past, a more adaptive response to an internal conflict, will be different for everyone. Whatever the individual regards as a better resolution to the past is the determinant that proves that a pattern of experience can change.

If, in the earliest stage of an Aries Moon, there was not enough security provided to attain a sense of independence and autonomy, then during the progressed Moon in Aries in the second cycle, or in the third, one could resolve this insufficiency by attaining the experience of autonomy through the support and security of a nurturing relationship later in life. The challenge of individuation requires an attuned relationship. It is also possible that, during a progressed Moon in Aries, someone who lacked a secure attachment in childhood will feels alone and may also feel that being alone is better than risking being vulnerable in a relationship. With enough help, psychological and spiritual, this pattern can change.

If the progressed Moon in Libra in the earliest stages of life was not a time of safety and dependency in an attachment relationship, then when the progressed Moon revisits Libra in its second and third cycle, the emphasis on partnership could be an expression of a difficulty in the earlier Libra stage. Dependency needs in relationship can either be feared or repressed. It is also possible for a person to manage dependency needs for the first time in healthy and rewarding relationships. The second and third cycles of the progressed Moon are fields that have both the imprint of the past and the opportunity for change in the future.

The following are general interpretations of the progressed Moon in the other ten signs as they may manifest in the second and third cycles. These descriptions focus on developmental problems that can be favorably resolved later in life under the positive influence of each sign. Of course this is not the outcome for everyone. But the point is to delineate the way the signs of the progressed Moon still retain real developmental implications even as they appear much later in life.

The challenge of a progressed Moon in Taurus in the second and third cycles lies in establishing security—providing it, accessing it, and maintaining it—either in concrete, physical, and material security or in the experience of being the provider of resources, emotional and material, to others. Internal emotional strength and stability are established early in life through consistency in the relationship with mother and other primary caregivers. If this experience of security was not established during the Taurus stage of early development, it can be achieved later in a life by choosing a life style that affords as much consistency, predictability, and material well-being as possible. In the second or third cycle, when an individual's progressed Moon is in Taurus, he or she will often become the rock for others in his or her life.

The progressed Moon in Gemini in the second and third cycles needs an arena for learning new skills, including communication skills, and for self-expression through all forms of art. There can be an opportunity to put feelings into words, or words into feelings that have been difficult to express. Getting the facts, the true story, the right information, is important during this progressed Moon cycle. Dualities may abound. There may be two of something—two siblings, two people, two kinds of endeavors. This duality can also show up as a desire or manifestation of twinship, the-you-and-me-together and we are exactly alike phenomenon. Relationships with siblings may be accentuated in later cycles, and early miscommunication, or lack of communication, can be resolved.

The progressed Moon in Cancer will trigger all issues involving attachment in the second and third cycles just as it did in the first, In fact, it will likely resurrect the kinds of attachment relationships that were formed early in life. If attachment was secure, then the experience during these cycles will likely be the same. However, anxious attachments formed in early childhood can be characteristic of relationships in later cycles, inviting an opportunity to heal patterns of relationship dysfunction. During the time the progressed Moon is in Cancer, one's mother may be prominent, affording an opportunity for mutual nurturing and/or to repair this primary relationship.

The progressed Moon in Leo in the second and third cycles depicts themes involving recognition, the nature of love relationships, or creative expression. If a person did not feel special or valued in the family, or early peer experience was shaming, then the challenge now would be to overcome feeling undervalued. The second and third cycle of the progressed Moon in Leo can become times for self-expression, creativity, and play.

The progressed Moon in Virgo in the second and third cycles is associated with learning and applying new skills that have practical purpose. Issues of health and well-being and the need to establish healthy routines can become the focus of these cycles. This placement may bring the need for rigorous self-discipline but perfectionism and self-criticism can become derailments. If, in the first cycle, emotional turmoil interfered with achieving intellectual and physical skills, then later cycles of the progressed Moon in Virgo can bring opportunities that build self-confidence through corrective experiences.

The progressed Moon in Scorpio in the second and third cycles generates themes of financial and emotional interdependencies. It can bring experiences of being tied closely to another person or to a group for financial and emotional survival. Power struggles in relationships can ensue as a response to feeling controlled in relationships. If emotional upheaval was characteristic of relationships during the earliest developmental stage of Scorpio, contradictory states of intense dependency and desire for control can characterize close relationships later in life. During the second and third cycles of the progressed Moon in Scorpio, the positive outcome would be the ability to let go of control in relationships, to manage the intensity of emotions that result from interdependencies and joint financial enterprise. The progressed Moon in Scorpio affords strength of purpose, commitment, and resolve.

The progressed Moon in Sagittarius brings a breath of fresh air. But this period, during a second and third cycle, can bring mixed blessings. If the earliest experience of the Sagittarius form of maturation was one without boundaries, too much freedom, too little guidance, and too much risk, then the progressed Mood in Sagittarius can feel overwhelming. In this stage, there can be a pressure to accelerate, to overextend and, subsequently, get worn out. However, managed well later in life, this Sagittarius experience can be revised with spiritual renewal, and aspirations that are more grounded in self-awareness. The second or third time around can build the capacity to balance risk with good judgment and forethought.

The progressed Moon in Capricorn in its second and third cycles requires an acceptance of limits, the limits defined by one's internal rules or boundaries, or the limits imposed by external circumstances. Fear and anxiety can arise during the second or third cycle of the progressed Moon in Capricorn, especially if the earliest developmental experience of Capricorn was one of insecurity and self-doubt. One must go slowly and cautiously, step by calculated step, to build or re-build confidence in oneself. The ability to be in a position of authority can shore up earlier insecurity. Being competent in a role of responsibility is self-empowering and healing in the second and third cycles of the progressed Capricorn Moon.

The progressed Moon in Aquarius seeks unique experiences and new involvements that expand one's consciousness. This period may also open up freedom of self-expression and a new and positive perspective about people and life. Finding the right people, the right friendships, in the second and third cycle of this progressed Moon is the key for this stage's enlightenment. This period may invite unusual people who can be delightfully eccentric or artistic, but who may also be lacking conventional social decorum. This may be a harmless characteristic of people who live outside of the rules defined by society. Or it may be that people who rebel against social conformity have serious malfunctions in their natures. If a person's very early social development was limited, and exposure to people and relationships lacking, the person going through the Aquarius stage must discriminate between people who expand his consciousness and people who close it down.

The progressed Moon in Pisces requires a capacity to surrender self-will to circumstances that are beyond the individual's control. In the second and third cycles, this stage can invite such an experience of helplessness and emotional upheaval that spiritual or psychological support is almost always a necessity. Our western society so values productivity that being unable to work or maintain a regular schedule of routines, can be regarded as failure. Particularly for men in our society, the inability to be productive, achieving, and having employment carries a weighty stigma. What needs to be emphasized during this period is that acceptance of one's state of inertia and of the need to retreat from life in some way is imperative for healing. Someone who, in the earliest progressed Moon in Pisces stage, was taught that emotions are not all right, that one must be rigidly in control of all aspects of one's life, might try to isolate during this time, to bear the confusion and pain alone. However, if in the first cycle, this Pisces stage brought comfort in relationships or in spiritual well being, then an individual in this stage will be strong enough to find multiple sources for healing.

All these descriptions for the progressed Moon distill chart interpretation to this one placement alone, *the sign and cycles of the Moon*. A horoscope is complex and the entirety of experience cannot be captured by just one astrological position. But having selectively isolating this one factor, it can now be re-integrated into the whole astrology chart.

The following charts illustrate how each time the Moon goes around, there can be an activation of a natal position or of a pattern that triggers unresolved issues. This can become an opportunity to experience, confront, and revise ways of responding to core issues in life. In addition, the examples that follow integrate other astrological data that are necessary in order to understand the significance of the whole planetary schema. The interpretations in all the forthcoming examples are a blend of astrology and developmental psychology. The principles of attachment theory and inter-subjectivity–the relational dependency in maturation–are central to understanding the developmental processes in these charts.

Chart 10 describes my client Mary. Her progressed Moon entered the second house in the sign of Sagittarius. Mary wanted to leave a job she had held for years because she wished to be a freelance artist and be her own boss. She also desired to break free from her marriage

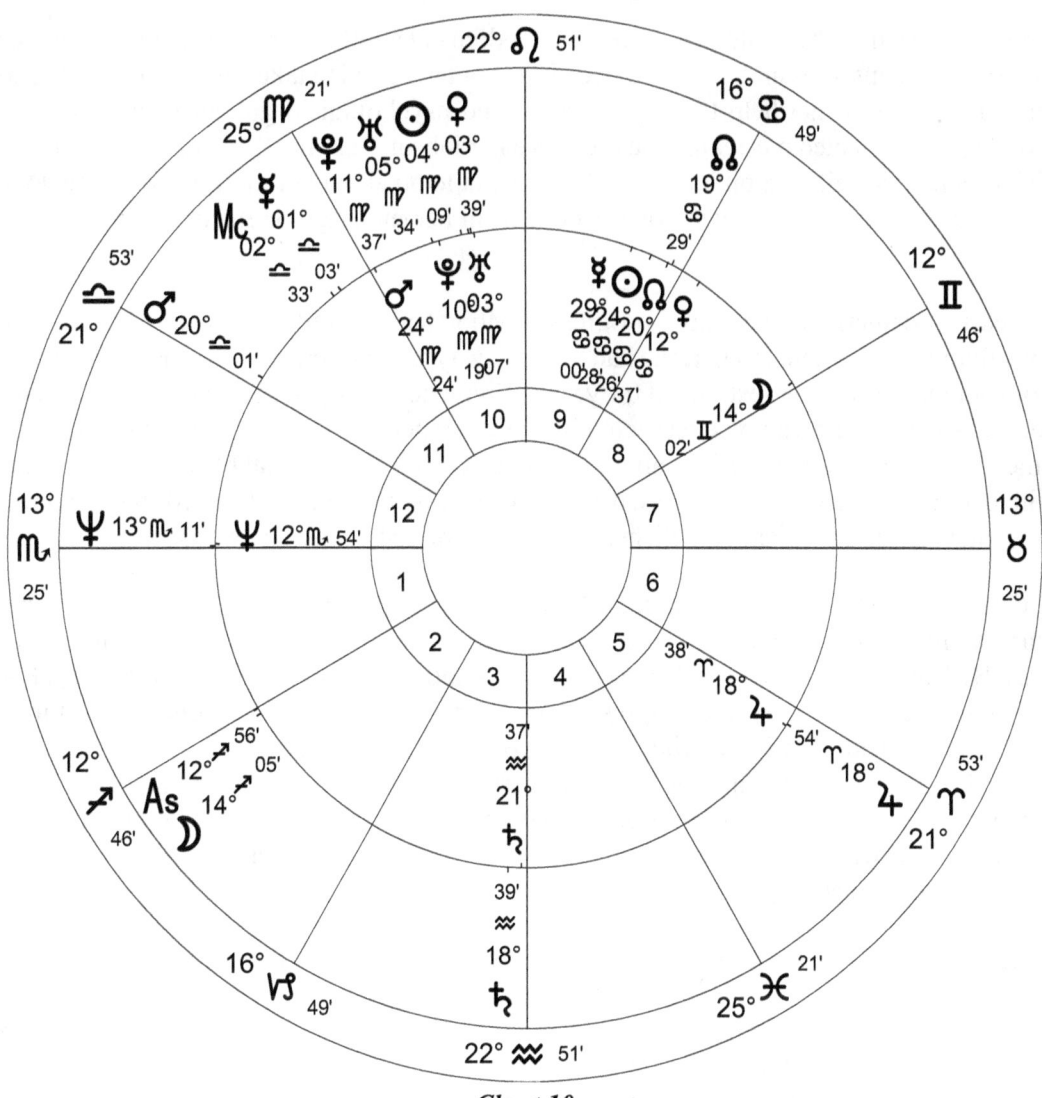

Chart 10.
Inner Wheel: Natal, July 17, 1963, 2:55 p.m. EDT, Huntington, New York
Outer Wheel: Progressed

and was on the verge of doing this during the month of our consultation. In addition her Sagittarius progressed Moon squares her natal Moon and the progressed Moon to birth Moon opposition, t-square to natal Uranus. This client had a very difficult relationship with her mother and twenty-seven years ago separated from her. It is this kind of rupture that her Sagittarius Moon was now pushing for again in its second cycle. My client, however, was in conflict, one part of her wanted to have this freedom but another part was uncertain. In order to arrive at a conscious and informed decision about her need to take flight, she decided, after our reading, to get help through spiritual and psychological guidance. Within a few months, she contacted me again. She did leave her job and felt that this had been a good decision. She was waiting a bit longer to decide what to do about her marriage because it was not clear whether her need was for freedom from her marriage or freedom from self-imposed restrictions.

Chart 11 depicts a client whose progressed Moon had entered Gemini at the time of our consultation. This client felt that she had to find a way to communicate with her two brothers from whom she had been estranged for years. Within her family her brothers had dominated her and she felt her own voice restricted by their competitive relationships with her. At the time of our consultation she was able to find her voice and to re-establish communication with her brothers. Here the progressed Moon in Gemini, the sign of the third stage of development, made communicating with her brothers her priority when she was a mature woman.

Chart 12 illustrates the progressed Moon in Pisces as it emerged in the chart of a man who had retired from his work as a doctor, not just because of age, but also because of illness. He had cancer and had undergone surgeries and was despairing of his recovery. Earlier in his life, during the same progressed Moon in Pisces, his wife left him and he turned to alcohol to deal with his feelings of loss. But now, during the third cycle of the progressed Moon in Pisces, although he was very depressed, he was finding solace in the company of two spiritual communities, a twelve-step program and his religion that he had abandoned earlier in his life. Through these spiritual involvements he said he gained strength and a sense of peace.

Chart 13 is that of a man who was well into his 40's, so his secondary progressed Moon was in its second cycle. He had been an architect but was unable to pursue his painting, a talent he had developed early in life. After a divorce destabilized him, he was compelled to re-establish his security, but in a different way than he was able to do before his divorce. Transiting Pluto was conjunct his natal Sun and he was undergoing radical changes through circumstances that befell him and challenges he was undertaking by his own choice. He moved into a new home to rear his two children and found work that gave him a predictable income without compromising his artistic needs. When his Moon had been in Taurus as a younger man, his desire and need for security and predictability limited his choices. Now, as a more mature man, this progressed Moon in Taurus gave my client the opportunity to create a foundation that afforded him financial security and more creative work as an architect that satisfied his artistic needs.

Repetitive Themes on the Circular Pathway of Development/87

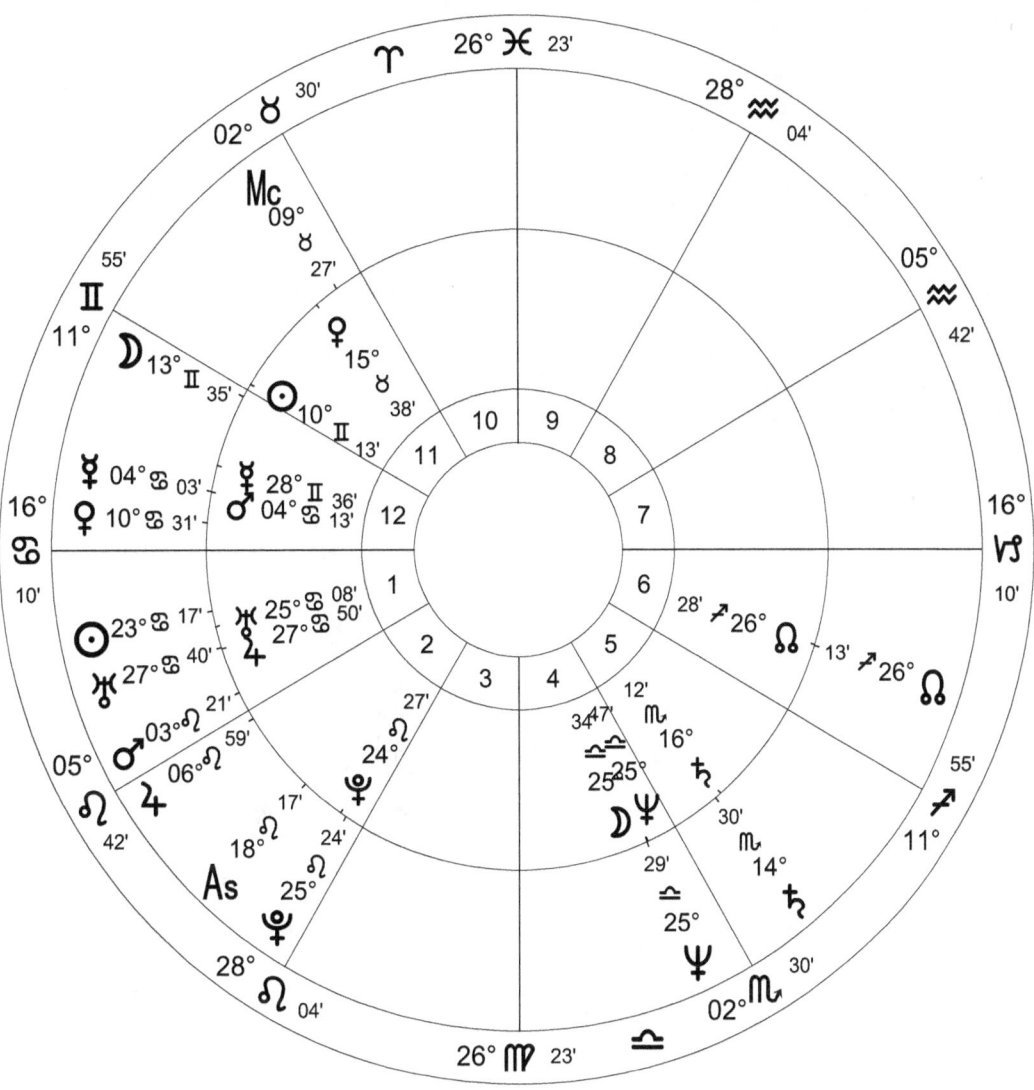

Chart 11.
Inner Wheel: Natal, June 1, 1955, 8:06 a.m., New York, New York
Outer Wheel: Progressed

88/The Progressed Moon Around the Zodiac

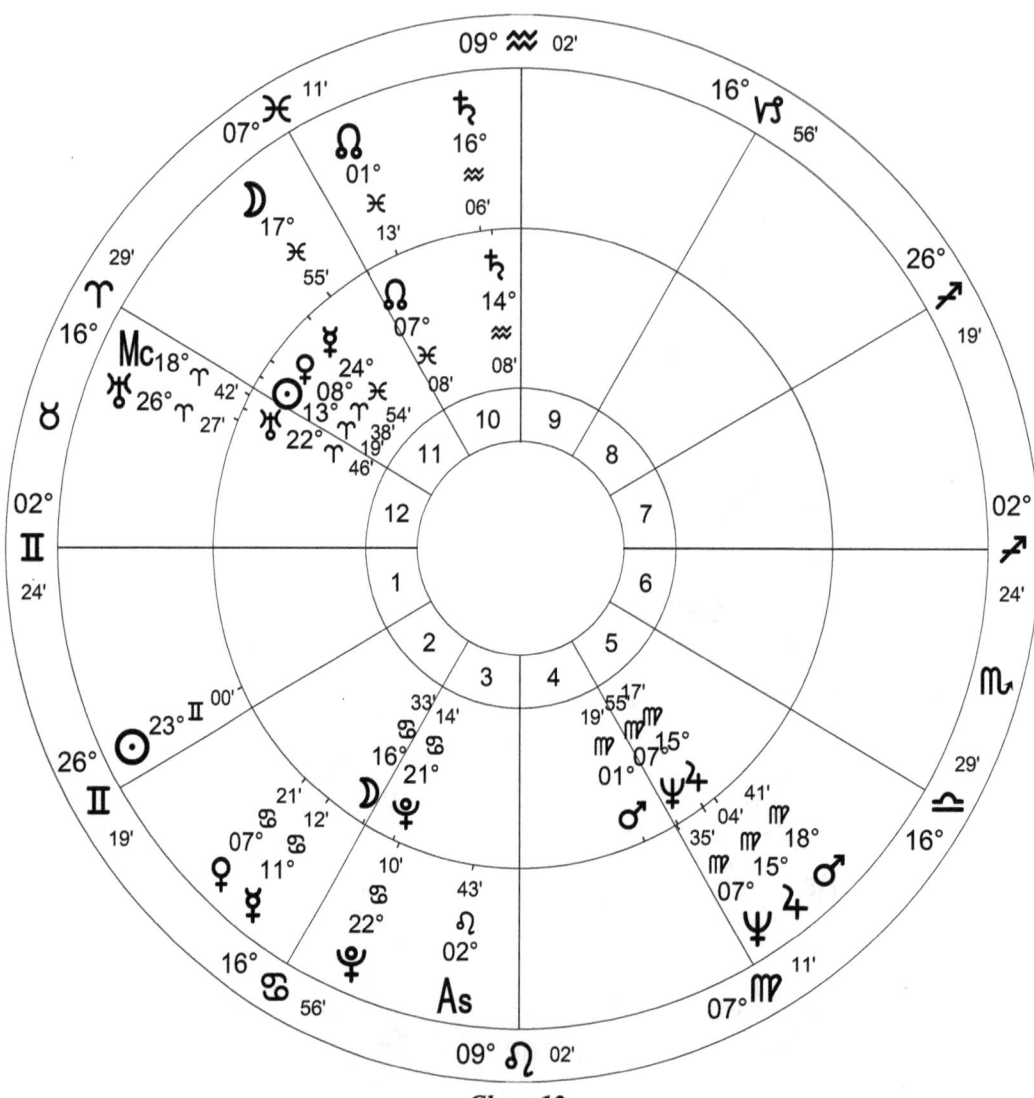

Chart 12.
Inner Wheel: Natal, April 3, 1933, 7:56 a.m., Brooklyn, New York
Outer Wheel: Progressed

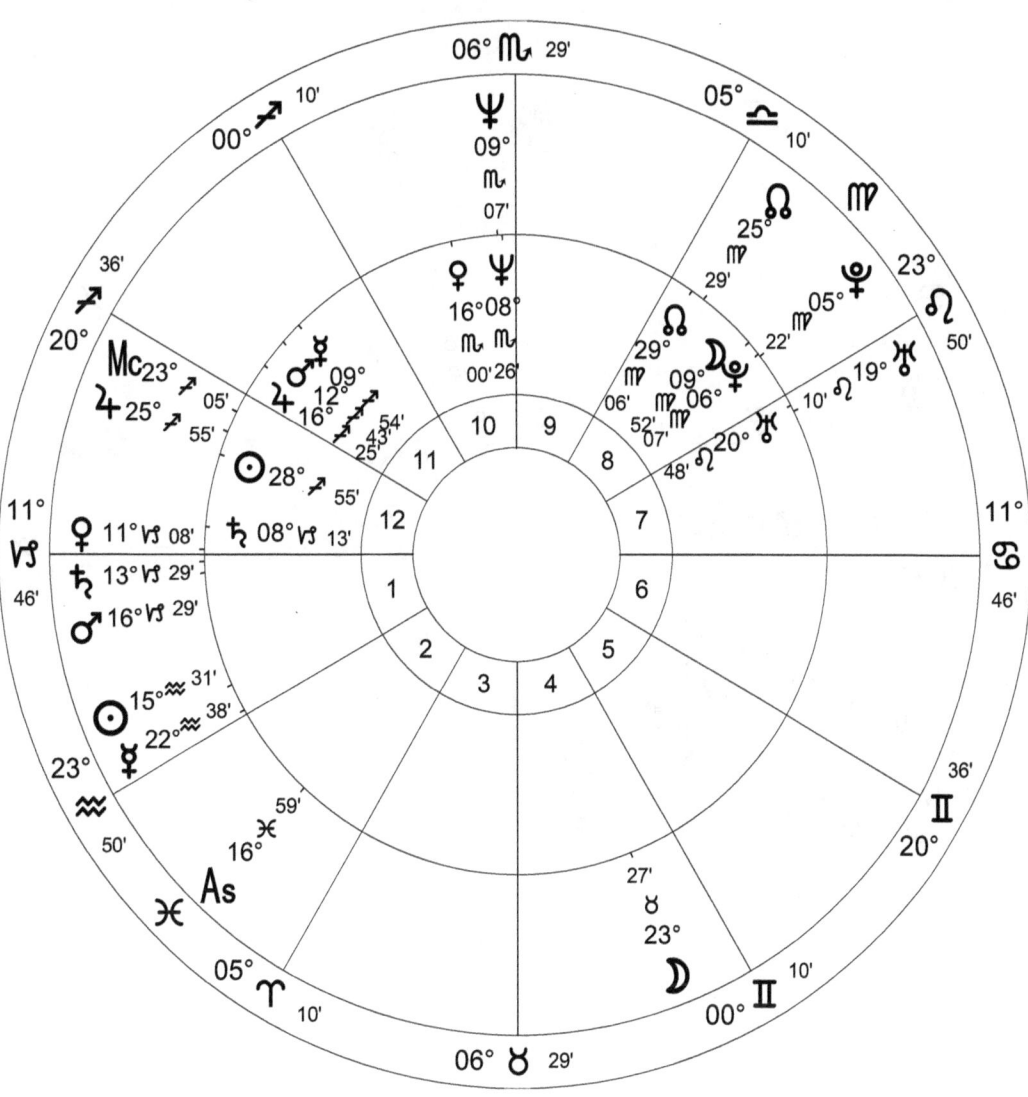

Chart 13.
Inner Wheel: Natal, December 21, 1959, 8:15 a.m. EST, Long Island City, New York
Outer Wheel: Progressed

90/The Progressed Moon Around the Zodiac

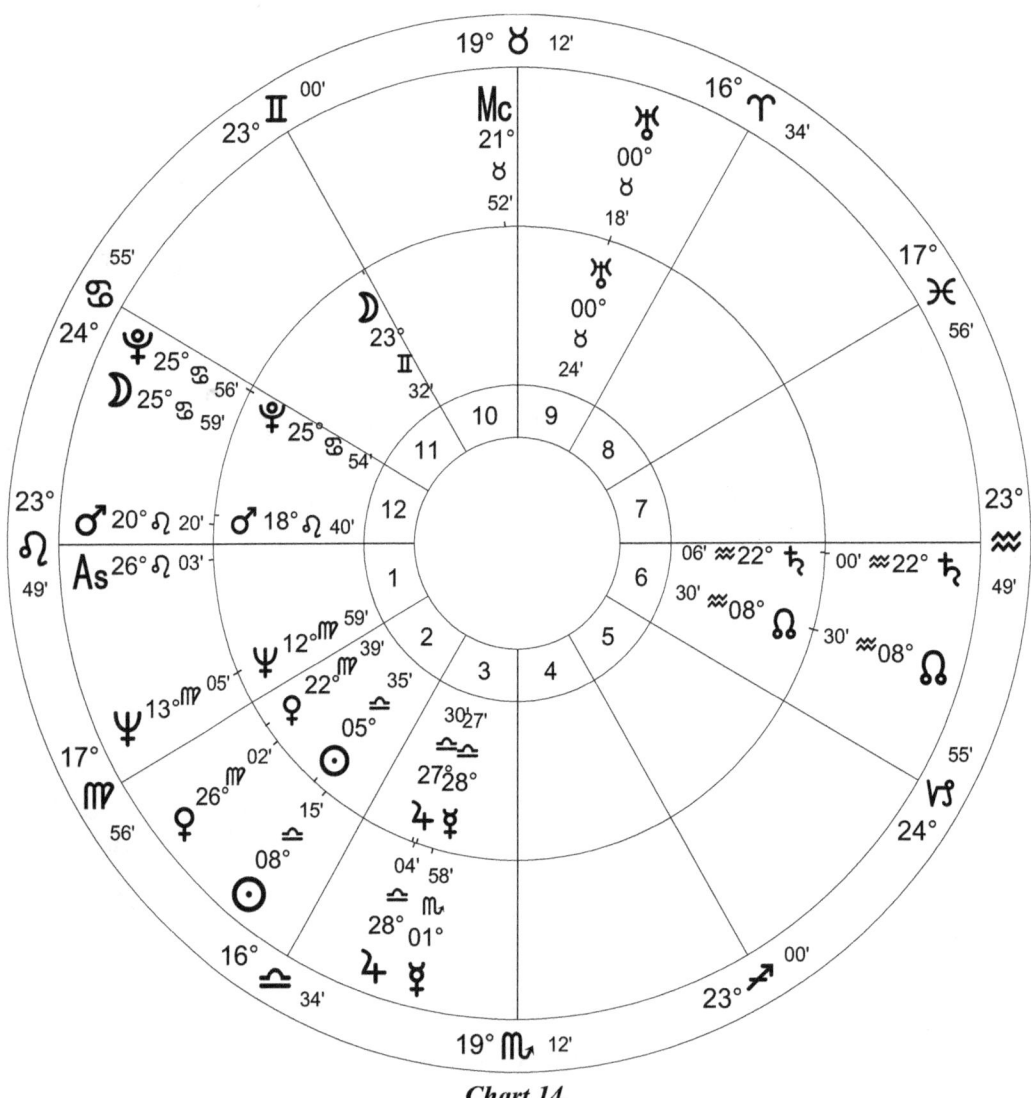

Chart 14.
Inner Wheel: September 29, 1934, 2:30 a.m. PST, Los Angeles, California
Outer Wheel: Progressed, Age 2

    Charts 14, 15, and 16 are of my client Jack. These depict the progressed Moon in Cancer in three cycles of the same sign. The progressed Moon in Cancer occurred in my client's twelfth house when he was two, thirty, and fifty-seven. When Jack was age two, the loss of his father, his mother's abandonment to alcohol, and his subsequent relationship with a rejecting stepfather set him up with many difficulties early in life. Here began a pattern of in-

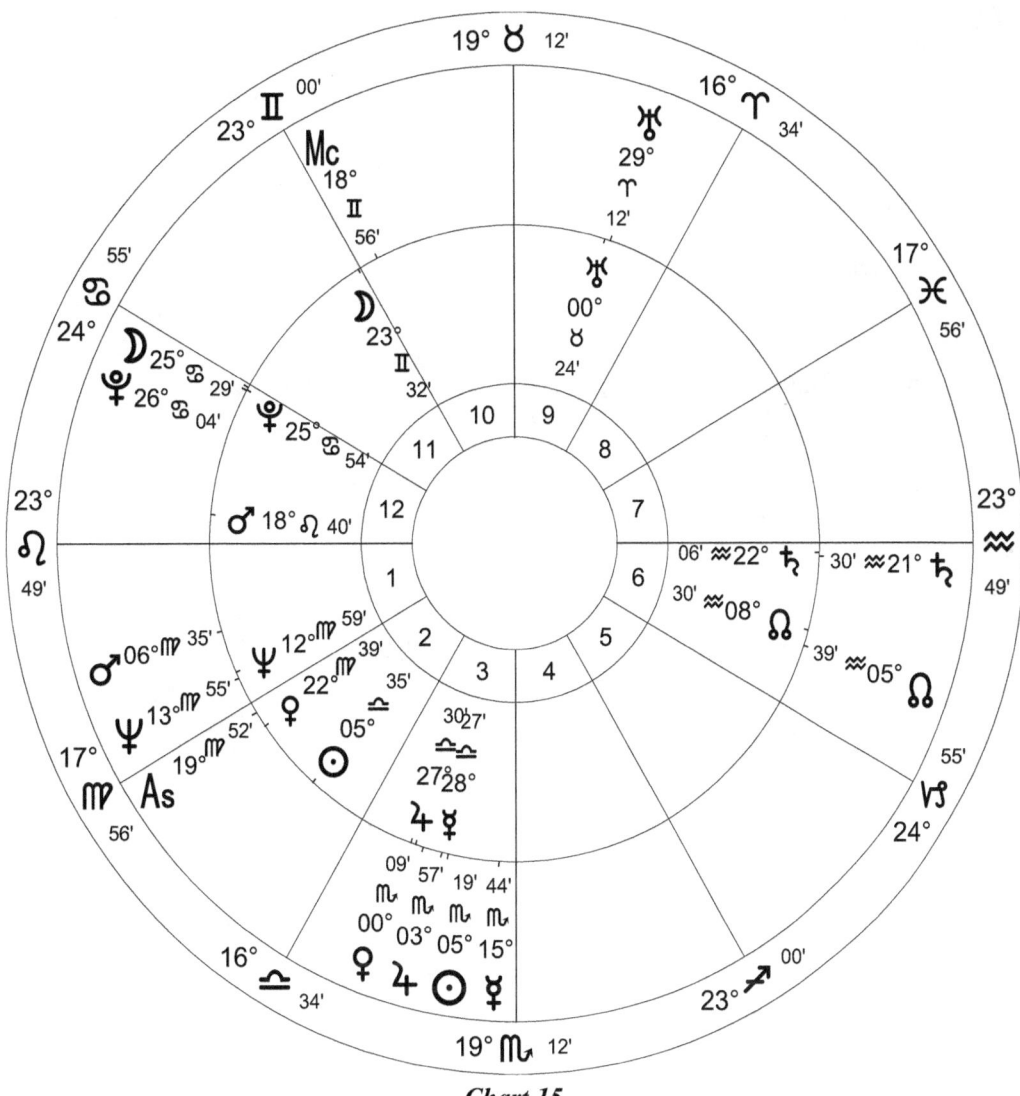

Chart 15.
Inner Wheel: September 29, 1934, 2:30 a.m. PST, Los Angeles, California
Outer Wheel: Progressed, Age 30

secure attachment. The second time the progressed Moon was in Cancer in the twelfth house, a rupture in attachment occurred again. Jack's marriage ended and he lost his home in the divorce. During the third passage of the Moon in Cancer in his twelfth house, however, he sought psychotherapy and was helped to cope with the losses in his life.

92/The Progressed Moon Around the Zodiac

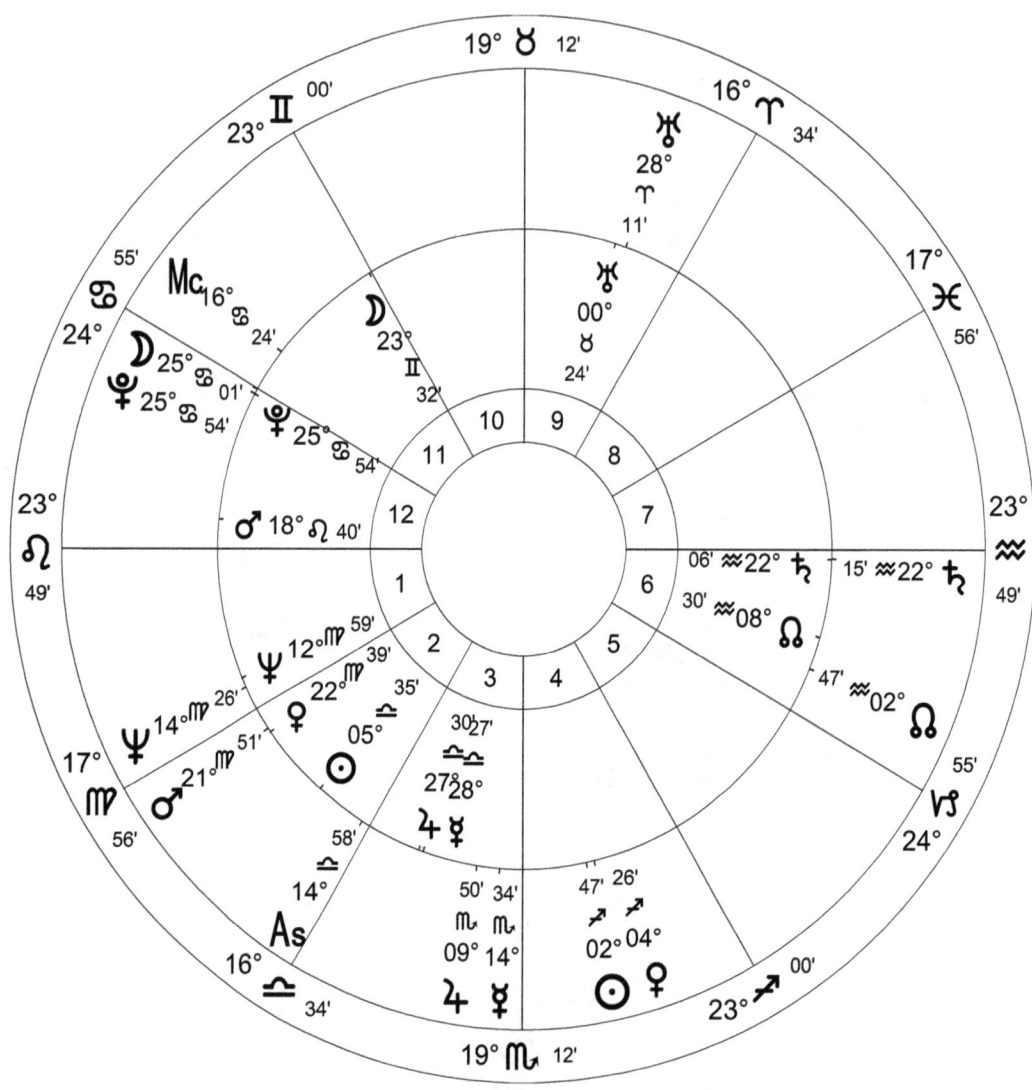

Chart 16.
Inner Wheel: September 29, 1934, 2:30 a.m. PST, Los Angeles, California
Outer Wheel: Progressed, Age 57

Repetitive Themes on the Pathway of Development/93

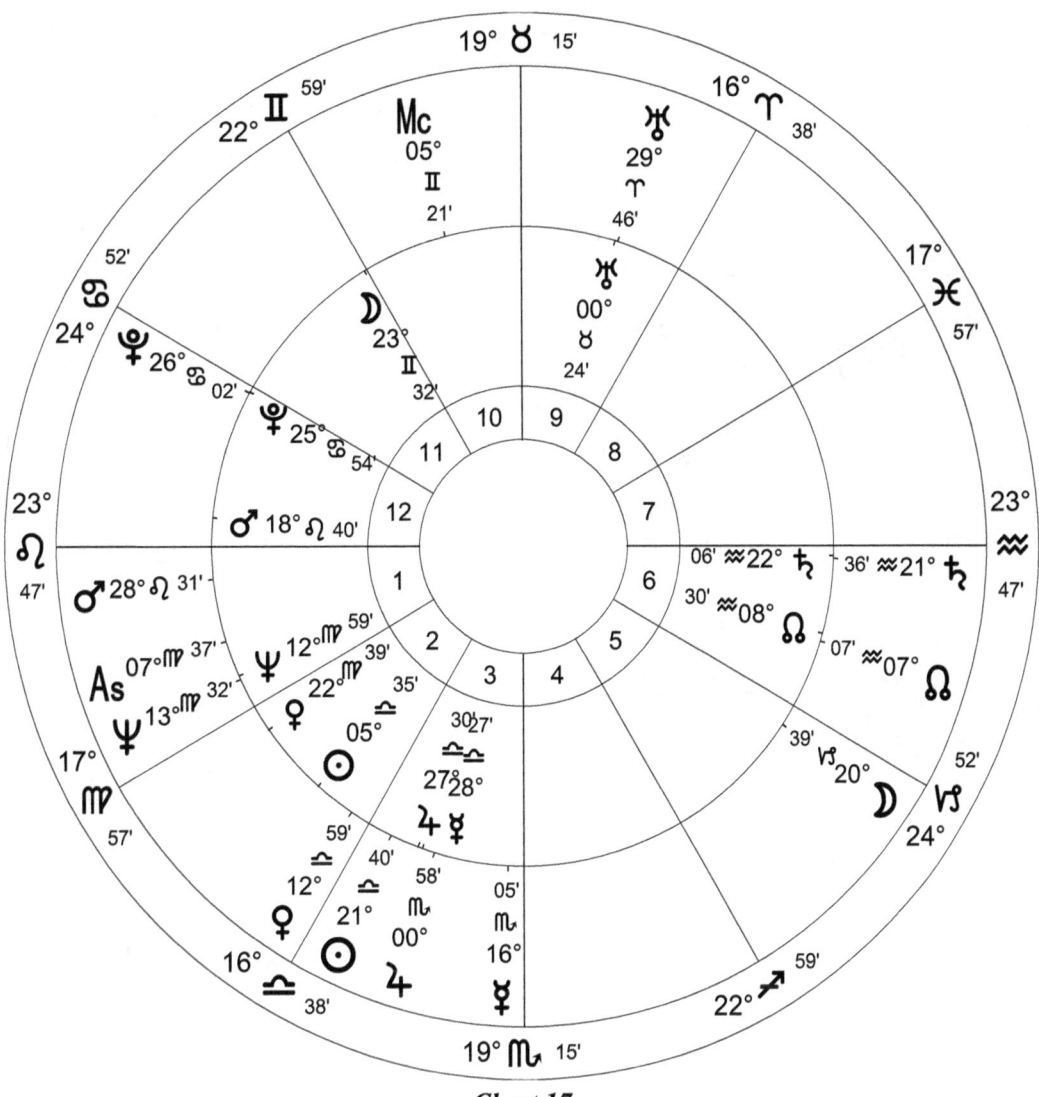

Chart 17.
Inner Wheel: September 29, 1934, 2:30 a.m. PST, Los Angeles, California
Outer Wheel: Progressed, Age 16

Charts 17, 18, and 19 illustrate the Moon's placement in the sign of Capricorn in the fifth house three times in this same client's life. This progressed Moon traveled through his fifth house when he was sixteen, forty-three, and seventy years old. The first time the Moon was in Capricorn Jack felt left out of a group, the cool group of friends he wanted to belong to, and his family's financial and social limitations restricted his social world. At the critical

94/The Progressed Moon Around the Zodiac

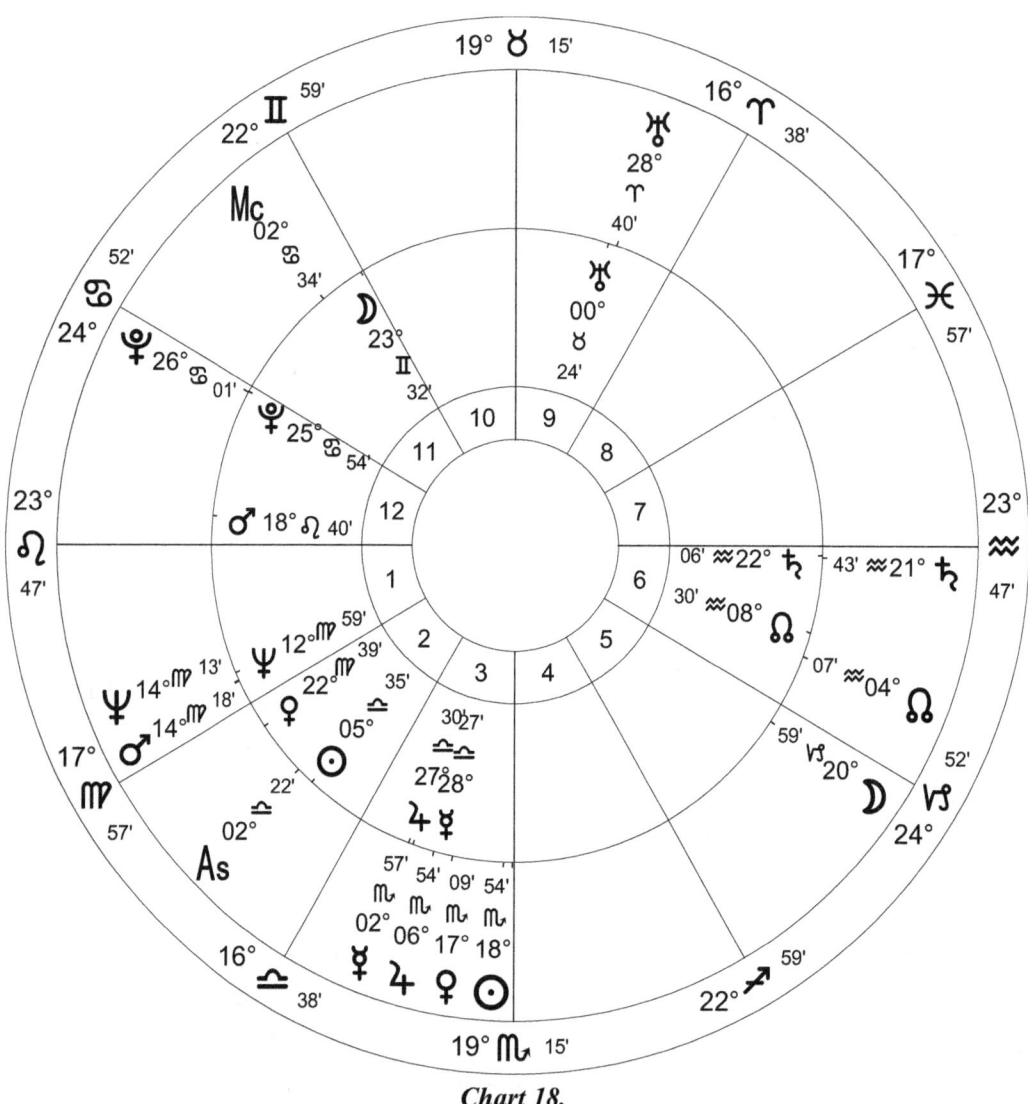

Chart 18.
Inner Wheel: September 29, 1934, 2:30 a.m. PST, Los Angeles, California
Outer Wheel: Progressed, Age 43

age of adolescence, this had considerable impact on his self-esteem. At age forty-three Jack was working professionally as an actor but was troubled because he felt that his agents were limiting his career advancement by not submitting him for parts in feature films. He left his agents, later regretting this decision. The third time the progressed Moon was in Capricorn, Jack went with the program. In fact he joined a twelve-step program and was working the

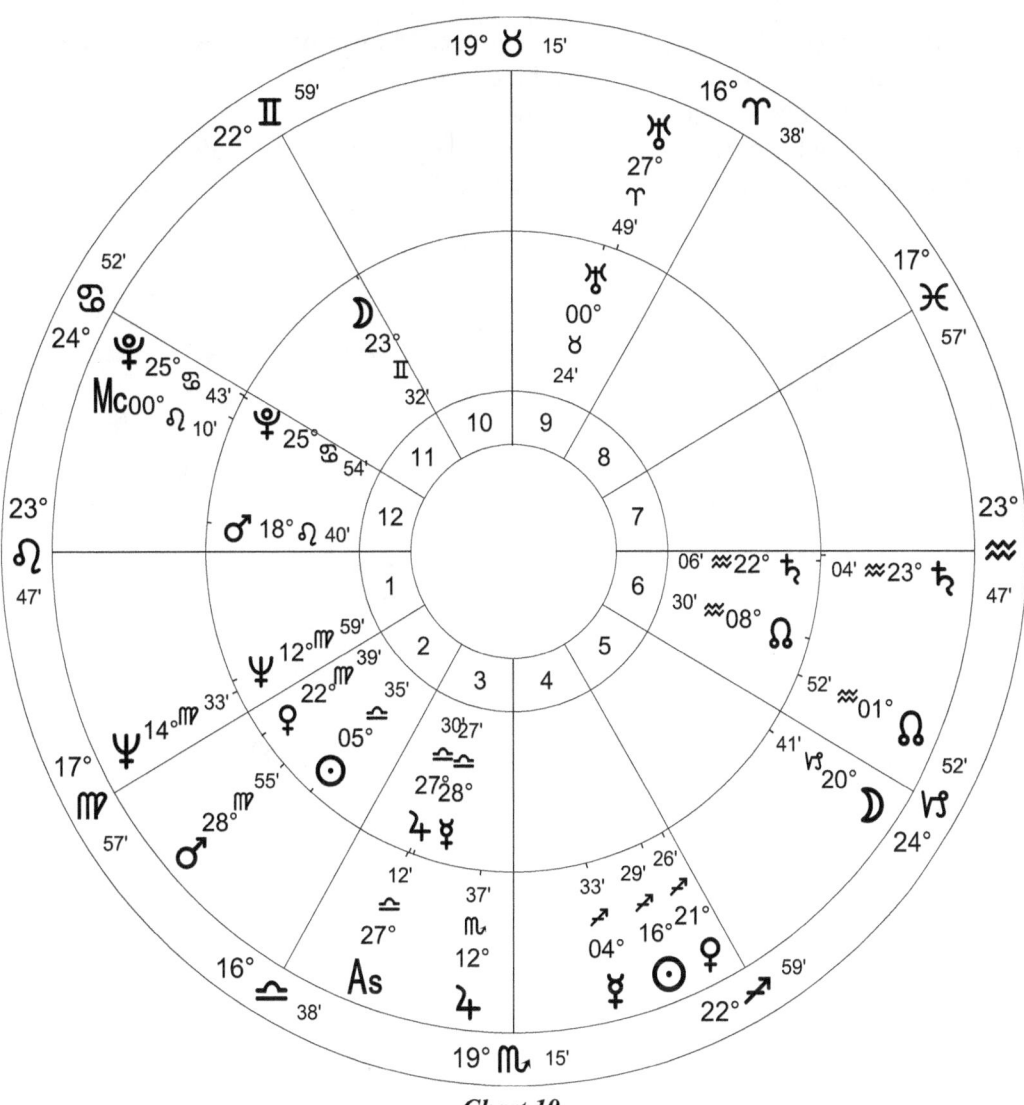

Chart 19.
Inner Wheel: September 29, 1934, 2:30 a.m. PST, Los Angeles, California
Outer Wheel: Progressed, Age 70

steps, and following the guidelines. This program gave him a spiritual foundation as well as a group of friends with whom he identifies. The shift from dependency upon alcohol for self-regulation to dependency upon a spiritual program for self-regulation is a developmental quantum leap.

Both the second and third cycles of the progressed Moon provide cues for understanding developmental change. As it travels around the zodiac, the Moon continues to operate as a relational system, often bringing opportunities to revise old scripts. By grasping the challenges that a sign of the progressed Moon poses, it is possible for an individual to gain mastery of a developmental theme that once caused difficulty or pain in his or her life.

Chapter Ten

Order and Chaos: Universal Patterns of Development

The progressed Moon has captured the attention of several prominent astrologers. Brian Clark, in "The Progressed Moon: Mnemosyne's Recollections,"[1] honors this cycle, its repetitive themes, and its significance as a mirror of the development of the human psyche. He describes the importance of the "initiatory" cycle (first twenty-seven and a third years) and highlights that the critical points in the cycle are the progressed Moon's square and opposition to the natal Moon and then the lunar return itself. He explains that "the key for understanding the progressed Moon is in its unraveling the ancient images and traditions that honored her and becoming familiar with the goddesses who personified her attributes." He also explains how the three cycles of the Moon are presided over by three goddesses: Artemis during the first lunar revolution because she rules the untamed forces of nature, Mnemosyne during the second cycle because she rules memory and the capacity to invoke prior emotional experiences, and Hecate Triformis during the third and last full lunar rotation because she incorporates heaven and earth and the underworld and so represents the capacity to stand at the crossroads of three worlds, to embrace them before passage to death and rebirth.

In *The Astrological Moon*[2], Darby Costello writes that "the progressed Moon's cycle reveals the unfolding story of emotional development" and "each succeeding sign and house it enters symbolizes new experiences and people." She illustrates how in its first cycle, the progressed Moon is tightly connected to the Saturn cycle and that both are mutually dependent on each other for a foundation of growth. She describes the inter-relationship between self and others on the course of development, and explains how the Moon, even as it separates immediately from its birth position, carries physical and emotional memory of the primary relationship with mother; yet it simultaneously symbolizes the reaching out to other experiences and other people that will shape ongoing development. On the theme of crucial junctures of the progressed Moon to its own natal position, Costello's work details the repeating themes associated with the angles that the progressed Moon makes to the natal Moon, always signifying important dimensions of attachment and separation.

Gloria Star, in *Developmental Crises in Childhood*, urges parents to watch the cycle of the progressed Moon to determine important periods of change in a child's life and that the sign of the Moon indicates the child's emotional focus.[3] "The external event is not as important as the fact that the child is experiencing a new emotional level of himself when the progressed Moon moves into the next sign." Different aspects of self are selected for growth as the Moon shifts from sign to sign, house to house, into aspect and out of aspect with the natal Moon's position.

Stephen Arroyo, in *Astrology, Karma and Transformation*[4], asserts that the progressed Moon is an especially valuable tool in timing and describing the area of life experience that is of greatest concern and consequence. He also emphasizes that the placement can have multiple meanings, those activating response patterns of the past, and those that invite new relationships, circumstances, and new avenues for human growth.

All these astrologers speak of the theme of attachment when referring to the Moon as the symbol for development. They express the nature of attachment when they allude to the way relationships continue to affect development on the repeating wheel of life. For each astrologer mentioned, the secondary progressed Moon reflects the activating processes of development, those pre-timed on the clock of both astrological cycles and biology, and those that arise spontaneously through interpersonal experiences.

There are interesting overlaps between the standard model of development in western astrology and the lunar return model. In the standard model, for example, at age two, Mars returns to its natal position. This coincides with the time of the "terrible two's." The reason for the terrible two's is that the toddler asserts his separateness with the word no, either verbally or in oppositional behavior. This form of self-assertion correlates with the end of the first stage of development in the lunar return theory, the stage of Aries, the sign ruled by Mars, the planet of self-assertion. At age three, Jupiter's influence dominates the world of the toddler. This corresponds to the second stage in the lunar return theory, the stage of Taurus. During this period, the exploration of the world that is governed by Jupiter is accomplished in a Taurus way—through the body (touch, feel, locomotion) and testing the physical boundaries of safety and danger. Age six in the standard developmental model of planetary cycles also comes under the province of Jupiter. In the lunar return theory, this Jupiter cycle occurs at the end of the third stage of Gemini in which the full expansion of language skills, writing skills, and imaginative play is evident. Age seven is the first Saturn square, and in the lunar return model, reason and awareness of reality are part of the fourth stage of Cancer because this is the phase in which a child, through the father, has learned to accept his own limits and to become more realistic in general. The table below references the stage of development in the lunar return theory that corresponds to the age of the planetary cycle. The cross-references between the two become apparent.

Age	Planet	Key Phrase	Lunar Return Theory
2	Mars	Anger/oppositional behavior	Aries/Taurus Stage
3	Jupiter	Exploring the world	Taurus Stage
6	Jupiter	Expansion of language skills	Gemini Stage
7	Saturn	Age of reason	Cancer Stage
9	Jupiter	Increase in cognitive abilities	Leo Stage
12	Jupiter	Expansion of social awareness	Virgo Stage
13	Uranus	Puberty and rebellion/individuation	Virgo Stage
14	Saturn	Social and moral responsibility	Libra Stage
15	Jupiter	Greater intimacy in relationships	Scorpio Stage
18	Jupiter	Need for freedom	Sagittarius Stage
21	Saturn/Jupiter	New social responsibilities	Capricorn Stage
24	Jupiter	Greater social networks	Aquarius Stage
27⅓	Moon	Full emotional growth cycle	Pisces/Aries Stage
28	Uranus	New awareness of individuality	Aries Stage
29½	Saturn	Sense of maturity, inner strength, endurance	Taurus Stage

The lunar return model of development follows the cycles of the progressed Moon, and also parallels both phases of human growth in psychology, and cycles of growth depicted by astrological planets.

In the lunar return model, each natal Moon initiates its own course of development, commencing with its sign at birth, and ending with the sign preceding it, before contacting its original position again. Therefore, each sign of the zodiac begins a path of development for twelve different sequences. And, for all, the Moon will initiate these astrological sequences with its sign position at birth. There are multiple factors that make each person's path unique, regardless of their generic form. Twelve paths of development can be identified and the sequence of development by sign will always be the same, regardless of the many variations in timing and quality of development that exists from person to person.

Each one of these twelve paths begins with a motive delineated by the sign of the natal Moon. This motive, derived from the sign, describes the strongest emotional needs that compel fulfillment through experience or relationship. Every path then proceeds to pursue a course of development designed to achieve this motive. Every path ends in a symbolic Pisces stage with the progressed Moon in the sign that precedes its natal sign position. This last stage, before the lunar return, regardless of the sign, often requires some kind of acceptance or surrender to one aspect of life. But this stage always precedes a new beginning, where hopes and dreams can be born again.

For the purpose of this map of twelve paths of development, the whole sign that precedes the sign of the natal Moon expresses the intended meaning about endings and surrender before the dawn of the next lunar cycle. In reality, however, the end of a lunar cycle generally culminates with the same sign of the natal Moon. If one were born, for example, with the Moon at 18 Aquarius, then the Moon in Aquarius from zero to seventeen degrees would actually precede the lunar return; Aquarius would thus represent part of the last stage of development before the lunar return. It may be helpful to assess both the sign preceding the natal Moon and the sign of the natal Moon to ascertain whether one or both better describe the nature of the closing of the cycle.

The Moon at birth parallels the natural order of development, with every sign corresponding with a traditional stage of growth in developmental psychology. For the Aries Moon person, conditions in the early relationship with mother promote an unusual degree of self-reliance and independence, for better or for worse. Because the Aries Moon at birth coincides with the first Aries stage, all the themes of development in the first cycle of life are consistent with the stages of development themselves. Even if there is some divergence, depending on the degree of the natal Moon, the cycle will end with the progressed Moon in Pisces, the sign that requires surrender and faith. It is necessary to accept some closure to a life experience before again embarking on the journey of development.

The Taurus Moon signifies the importance of security, emotionally and physically, and as a result of this in the first relationship experience, the need for security will play an important role for the lifetime. All stages of development that follow before the lunar return will end with the progressed Moon in Aries, suggesting that something about identity brings crisis. Finding oneself apart from the rest of the world requires an internal quest of self-acceptance before beginning the journey of development again with the Moon in Taurus.

The Gemini path begins with the importance of perception—mental, visual, and kinesthetic. Reading, writing, and self-expression may be selected for greater emphasis because of the relationship with mother. This cycle ends with the progressed Moon in Taurus, meaning that surrender involves dealing with the reality of security needs that may have been ignored or uncared-for in the years preceding. And then the cycle begins anew with the Moon again in Gemini.

The path of Cancer highlights the attachment relationship itself, any breaches in it, or the unusually strong identification with mother and mothering that results from the earliest attachment relationship. This journey ends with the progressed Moon in Gemini. A means of communication may be thwarted, or communication might be imperative in order to put feelings into words, or words into action , and then start again with the Moon in Cancer.

The natal Moon in Leo establishes early in life the need to be admired. Something about this becomes keenly important as a result of the relationship with mother. And this cycle closes with the progressed Moon in Cancer, where themes of insecurity and co-dependency will be confronted. Needs for nurturing must be acknowledged and healed before attaining the outward confidence to express oneself with the Moon's cycle beginning again in Leo.

The natal Virgo Moon begins its path with the need to be of service and to mend all that is flawed or broken in mother during the first cycle, and then in other people and in material artifacts in the second and third cycles. This path culminates with the progressed Moon in Leo, where the experience of love, acknowledgement, honor and recognition may cause pain because it was sought from one who could not give it, or the price for receiving it was too high. Surrender to the reality of the loss of love or recognition is necessary before resuming service and productivity again under the Moon sign of Virgo.

Libra initiating the path of development brings dependency needs and the need for partnership, into high profile through the relationship with mother. The Libra Moon path also sensitizes an individual to art and beauty and to perception in general. It always culminates in a progressed Moon in Virgo stage where endeavors that demand skill and service require great sacrifice.

Scorpio at the helm of development through its Moon-sign placement at birth brings intensity to the struggle for survival. The theme of emotional self-control is often important for this Moon placement. To the extent that deep emotions can be controlled, this person is a master of containment and depth, working with internal willpower for better or for worse. At the end of this pathway will be the Moon in Libra, in which a significant relationship undergoes a transition or dependency needs in relationships may surface in order to be healed.

With the natal Moon in Sagittarius initiating the chain of development, the quest for freedom of thought, action, and self-expression is vital. Before this Moon reaches its lunar return the person may experience, in the sign of Scorpio, a relationship or a situation that challenges the essence of his or her being. While there may have been emotional or financial ties to this person or situation, only when the bonds are broken can the developmental cycle begin again.

Capricorn's developmental path sensitizes a person to feelings of insecurity and a desire for control and achievement. The developmental path cycles around only after passing through the sign of Sagittarius where one is set free, often not of one's choice. The Sagittarius stage requires taking risks and circumstances may require greater expansion of one's internal spiritual base.

When Aquarius is at the beginning of the developmental cycle (in its natal sign and prior to its natal degree), a tendency to detachment and experimentation draws this person on a mission, away from controlling and overpowering relationships. But before the lunar return, the individual must encounter some situation that puts the controls back on and asks that he or she place limits on the kinds of ventures sought, or requires an acceptance that sometimes goals can only succeed in small and cautious ways.

Pisces enfolds all the rest of the signs because it is the last sign in the zodiac. The sign is cumulative in emotional development in that it has taken in all lessons from all preceding signs. The person with this placement is inclined to absorb the emotional states of others, an effect from early childhood, resulting in a tendency to withdraw or internalize and split off overwhelming emotional states. This Moon will make its lunar return after the Moon goes through the Aquarius stage. Here there may be an encounter with new ideas and innovative experiences through friendship and group involvement. These may require experimentation in something novel, or an acceptance of something or someone out of the norm before returning to the familiar emotional zone of the Pisces Moon.

Focusing on one symbol in a chart and assigning it an exact meaning is artificial because other factors influence interpretation and there is never only one meaning for a specific placement. Meaning arises holistically, on multiple tracks.

The lunar return model provides a new perspective to human development in astrology. It integrates developmental psychology, a study not often utilized with astrology. Traditional astrology has offered other useful developmental models. These include the lunation cycle (Rudhyar)[5], the Saturn and the progressed Moon cycle (Costello)[6], and evolutionary astrology[6] which builds its developmental hypothesis on the progressed cycle of the Moon's nodes that ascend from the nadir around the wheel of the horoscope. The Vedic dasha system is a developmental system that differentiates periods of growth into nine stages and predicts important timing of transitions from one period of development to the next. And the interweaving of all cycles that Alexander Ruperti illustrates in *Cycles of Becoming* constitutes a rich developmental model. In all systems of astrology, growth occurs in cycles.

All of nature has processes of self-organization and change. From the quantum level to the molecular, from the molecular to the microbe, from the microbe to human, and from human interaction to the symbolic/archetypal plan of astrology, this change is a result of the influx of new information into stable but open systems. This awareness is embraced by disciplines such as ethology, neuroscience, biology, and non-linear dynamics. They all describe the way systems in nature are both inherently self organizing within their internal structures and are simultaneously changed by their external environments. Systems that survive must reorganize themselves based upon the external environments that they depend upon for survival. The molecules that formed us last month are not the same ones that are constructing us today. Yet we retain a consistent internal and external form even in the midst of these changes. "As living organisms we are destined to interact and exchange with our environments. It is how we sustain life, self-regulate and expand ourselves."[7]

There are, however, different points of view in the social sciences about how much growth is predetermined by genes and how much is a result of the external effects of environment and relationships. Both will govern processes in the brain and translate into human behavior. Evolutionary psychology stakes its claim on the genetic inscriptions of evolution and the subcortical brain[8] that still governs man's primary motivations. Mankind is still on the savannah. Evolutionary psychologists do not deny the environmental influences and effect of primary relationships upon development, but put more emphasis on the imprint of evolution on motivation and behavior. According to their position, development is more the result of internal and inflexible predetermined structures of genes than to relational or environment conditioning. Also, these genetic inscriptions form closed circuits and cannot be changed.

But the position in the lunar return model is more complex. It is based upon an understanding of human growth that has integrated features of both predeterminism (in genetic inscriptions) as well as randomness and spontaneity (in dyadic interactions). Ultimately it may be that the difference between these two camps is marginal. Nature and nurture are mutually dependent, not separate and conflicting perceptions of the process of growth. Nature prepares the mother to nurture, whose nurturing, in turn, effects the nature of neuro-chemical balances in the infant's developing brain. The mother's capacity for transactions that effect, for example, opiate receptors in the brain (regulating pleasure) at critical stages of development, may not be random or spontaneous but bio-genetically directed[9].

What astrologers already know is that the internal and external are one and the same. That what is predetermined and what happens spontaneously can be captured in one symbol. In this way astrology operates according to the same principles of nature, as molecules and human beings and societies, but in a symbolic form. The astrology chart retains its inherent structure as it absorbs the energy that flows into its system symbolically, through progressions and transits. New forms of experience, and new meanings result from this. Dynamic systems are never in states of equilibrium and neither is the chart. Like the flow of water, currents of air, cloud formation, and even societies, the astrology chart is a dynamic system and the Moon in particular provides symbolic energy exchanges with positions in the chart that catalyze new information in random processes.

Because of the relative speed of the progressed Moon, the astrology chart is constantly open to unique and spontaneous changes that propel the sum of its symbols and patterns to new arrangements of meaning. Through the progressed Moon, the external information from the environment that feeds into the internal system of the chart, sparks new connections, responds to developmental needs, and integrates new and higher levels of complex information through natal, progressed and transiting patterns. Through the position of the Moon, new information constantly rearranges the system, on the representational level of the chart. Whether according to internal clocks or external circumstances, by random occurrence or through unifying patterns of cosmic cycles, the astrology chart reflects that the growth of all living systems—from unicellular microbes to planet Earth to human beings—is experience dependent. And the Moon is the primary symbol for this process.

One purpose of this book has been to advocate for an interdisciplinary approach to interpreting astrology, an approach that is not often used with astrology and yet it is compatible with it. An astrology chart can interpret development in the language of psychological growth and development in the language of spiritual growth. Another intent has been to present a perspective of understanding by isolating one placement, the progressed Moon, so that it can then be re-integrated with others patterns in the astrology chart.

Signs of the zodiac parallel stages of human growth described in developmental psychology. And development is holistic. The same capacities that mature in early cycles of growth mature during later cycles of growth, and cycles that encompass larger cycles of time. It is possible to see the same sequence of signs unfold between birth and eighteen months, as between birth to age six. In a similar way, all twelve stages from birth to the first lunar return are represented in the expanded cycle of the life span of birth to eighty-four years. Like concentric circles within circles, or fractals in mathematics, at whatever level development occurs, it mirrors the signs of the zodiac at different levels of organization.

The striking correspondence between models of growth in astrology and developmental psychology is not unique to just these bodies of knowledge. There is a replication of this same developmental model across other disciplinary lines. The arc of direction in all models is similar, not exact, from the personal to the universal. The twelve-step programs are developmental models that begin with a focus on self and move toward surrender of self-will to a higher power and then toward service to others. In the Yoga Sutra of Patanjali, who is credited with systematizing the knowledge of yoga more than two thousand years ago,[10] the path to self-realization moves from the external world of service to others, to the internal world of service to self, and then to the spiritual world of self transcendence.

No body of knowledge—astrology, developmental psychology, or the path to self-realization—had access to another in fashioning its developmental theory, so these models arose on their own. Somewhere, embedded in the universe, is perhaps an inherent pattern of development that becomes visible through different disciplines. The question arises as to whether this order is inherent first in nature and is then reflected through the psyche of man as he creates developmental paths in creative and spiritual pursuits or whether the order is enshrined in the archetypal patterns of the universe, and then reflected in nature. If there is a pattern of development inscribed in the universe, is it a feature of our local universe alone? Might it be a feature of the arrow of time, which is conceived by physicists as linear? Or might the pattern curve around at distances far beyond the mind's comprehension and be in fact circular, like this development model of the lunar return?

The structure of astrology suggests that there is a universal pattern of development beyond the bio-behavioral and psychological growth models of developmental psychology. There appear to be atemporal and acausal principles in nature and these two principles are expressed through symbols in astrology. These are 1) the law of equivalence; that which becomes already is, and 2) the law of synchronicity; that events seemingly separated by time and space, with no causal relationship, are connected and meaningful. In astrology every planetary cycle expresses the synergy of both these universal laws.

One of the hypotheses put forth here is that the pattern of human development that repeats across disciplinary lines is archetypal. This means that whatever appears preprogrammed—by genetics or according to the movement in time and space of planetary cycles—already exists as a timeless universal pattern. As astrologers we attempt to interpret the convergence of universal law and individual purpose for our clients. We try to apprehend the coexistence of both known time and space and the unknown and unknowable beyond time and space. As in any developmental stage theory, cycles of planets in astrology proceed in predictable order, but as astrologers we are aware that their predictability is archetypal and not oriented towards the physical. There is mystery in this. And as astrologers we attempt to interpret both the tangible and the mysterious simultaneously.

Endnotes

Introduction

"Chaos, or complexity, theory." Gleick, James. 1987. *Chaos: Making A New Science.* New York: Viking Penguin, Inc. pp 11-31.

"Systems Theory" General Systems Theory Biologist. 1952. Von Bertalanffy who proposed two principles essential for life: 1) organization—living systems bring wholeness or unity among interacting components into coherent functioning—the whole is greater that the sum of its parts—coherence comes from the inside; 2) primary activity—every systems internal mechanism for self maintenance—each living system is self organizing self correcting, self regulating; and 3) the whole is greater than the sum of its parts.

"Rupert Sheldrake's biomorphic field theory." Sheldrake, Rupert. 1989. *The Presence of the Past; Morphic Resonance and the Habits of Nature.* New York: Vintage Books.

"Neuroscience," Panskeep, Jaak. 1998. *Affective Neuroscience; The Foundations of Human and Animal Emotions.* N.Y.: Oxford Press, p. 9.

"Consilience, a synthesis of concepts and findings from a range of scientific disciplines." Siegle, Daniel J. 1999. *The Developing Mind; How Relationships and the Brain Interact.* New York: Guilford Press. p 2.

Chapter One

[1]"In psychology these models originated over a century ago and describe fundamental aspects of psychological growth—emotional, sexual, cognitive, moral, and linguistic." Crain, William. 2000. *Theories of Development; Concepts and Applications.* N.Y.: Prentice Hall, p.ix.

[2]"The entire time for all nine Dashas to complete their assigned duration is 120 years." Harness, Dennis. 2000. *Hindu Dasha System—Exploring Predictive Planetary Periods.* Anaheim, ISAR Conference 2000: Tape ISR20-054, Sun Recording Service.

[3]"Humanistic beliefs have been expressed throughout history any time human dignity and freedom of expression has been repressed." Crain, William. 2000. *Theories of Development; Concepts and Applications.* N.Y.: Prentice Hall, pp 361-368.

[4]"Self actualization." Humanistic psychology promotes man's quest for "self actualization." Pro-

posed by Abraham Maslow, it is a state of understanding one's true purpose in life. The humanistic philosophy affirms that the natural tendency of human nature is towards goodness and wholeness and the natural tendency of man is to develop in the direction of purpose and self realization. Carl Rogers and Abraham Maslow were the psychologists at the forefront of the humanist movement. Their approach begins with the assumption that human nature is essentially "good," that the person shares with all living organisms an "actualizing tendency . . . to grow, to develop, to realize its full potential." Crain, William. 2000. *Theories of Development; Concepts and Applications*. N.Y.: Prentice Hall p. 361-368.

[6]"Astrologers became connected with humanistic philosophy in the 1960s" through the work of Dane Rudhyar." Ruperti, Alexander. 2005. *Cycles of Becoming*. Santa Monica: Earthwalk School of Astrology. p. 7.

[6]"Rogers called this a "person" or "client-centered" approach to therapy." The humanistic perspective is phenomenological, i.e. how a person feels and experiences his life is more important than observations or interpretations about him. Crain, William. 2000. *Theories of Development; Concepts and Applications*. N.Y.: Prentice Hall p. 361-368.

[7]"He (Carl Jung) brought this same philosophy to his study of astrology." Hyde, Maggie. 1992. *Jung and Astrology*. Northampton, England.

[8]"Person-centered astrology." Rudhyar, Dane. 1976. *Person Centered Astrology*. New York: Aurora Press.

[9]"Astrology as the study of cycles becomes a study of the pattern or plan of what Jung called the individuation process revealing in symbolic language how each person can fully become what he potentially is." Ruperti, Alexander. 2005. *Cycles of Becoming*. Santa Monica: Earthwalk School of Astrology. p 27.

[10]"Bruno and Louise Huber also conveyed a humanistic view of astrology in *Astrological Psychosynthesis*." Huber, Bruno. (1996). *Astrological Psychosynthesis*. York Beach: Samuel Weiser, Inc.

Chapter Two

[1]"Examples of this are Montessori's learning theory, Bandura's social modeling theory, and Skinner's theory of conditioned responses." Crain, William. 2000. *Theories of Development; Concepts and Applications*. N.Y.: Prentice Hall, pp 170-213.

[2]"In all theories, growth is hierarchical, one level assimilated by the next at successively more complex levels." Crain, William. 2000. *Theories of Development; Concepts and Applications*. N.Y.: Prentice Hall, p 289.

[3]Crawling occurs for infants at about nine months and walking at about twelve months. "Child Development." Davies, Douglas. 1999. *Child Development*. N.Y: Guilford Press.

[4]"Some stage models of development, like Piaget's cognitive development and Kohlberg's moral development." Crain, William. 2000. *Theories of Development; Concepts and Applications*. N.Y.: Prentice Hall, pp 110-160.

[5] "Whatever constitutes normal infant to adult development was not a subject of analysis." Stern, Daniel N. 1985. *The Interpersonal World of the Infant*. N.Y.: Basic Books, pp. 20-23.

[6] "Alexander Ruperti advocates observing the cycles of Jupiter and Saturn together, as their influences inter-relate with periods of growth and expansion, and acceptance of limits and challenges of responsibility." Ruperti, Alexander. 2005. *Cycles of Becoming*. Santa Monica: Earthwalk School of Astrology, p. 47.

[7] "The same occurs again at ages fifteen, eighteen, and twenty-one. Jupiter's influence is felt again, every three years until age twenty-four when another full Jupiter return is complete." Star, Gloria. 2000. *Astrology & Your Child: A Handbook for Parents*. St. Paul; Llewellyn Publications, p. 271.

[8] "Margaret Mahler." Crain, William. 2000. *Theories of Development; Concepts and Applications*. N.Y.: Prentice Hall, pp. 297-311.

[9] "Erik Erikson." Crain, William. 2000. *Theories of Development; Concepts and Applications* N.Y.: Prentice Hall, pp. 271-297.

[10] "This is the work of political and social journalist Gail Sheehy." Sheehy, Gail. *New Passages*. New York: Bantam.

[11] "Egocentrism is the thinking modality of toddlers, the 'me,' 'mine,' 'I want' and the need for immediate gratification." Piaget's cognitive development. Crain, William. 2000. *Theories of Development; Concepts and Applications*. N.Y.: Prentice Hall, pp. 110-147.

[12] "Glennys Lawton, in her work with the Moon and childhood development, associates early attachment patterns with lunar aspects to outer planets." Lawton, Glennys. 2003. *Attachment Styles and Adult Relationships*. Anaheim, ISAR Conference, 2003: Tape ISR23-041, Sun Recording Service.

[13] "There is an astrological model of development that correlates astrology with a lifespan theory and was formulated by astrologer and psychotherapist Glenn Perry, Ph.d." Perry, Glenn. *Twelve Steps to Enlightenment* (available on tape). San Raphael: Association of AstroPsychology.

[14] "Each cycle could be considered the lifespan of one specific type of entity retaining specific characteristics, biological or psycho-spiritual, during the entire cycle." Rudhyar, Dane. 1976. *Person Centered Astrology*. New York: Aurora Press, p. 103

Chapter Three

[1] "PET Scan and MRI." Moskowitz, M., Monk, C., Kaye, C., Ellman, S., editors. 1997. *The Neurobiological Basis for Psychotherapeutic Intervention*. New Jersey: Jason Aronson, Ltd., pp. 35-36.

[2] Schore, Allan. 1994. *Affect Regulation and the Origin of the Self; The Neurobiology of Emotional Development*. Hillsdale, NJ. Earlbaum, pp. 64-67.

[3] "At birth the infant brain is the most undifferentiated organ in the body." Siegle, Daniel J. 1999. *The Developing Mind; How Relationships and the Brain Interact*. New York: Guilford Press, p. 14

[4] Schore, Allan. 1994. *Affect Regulation and the Origin of the Self; The Neurobiology of Emotional Development*. Hillsdale, NJ.: Earlbaum, pp, 64-67, p 20.

[5]"Neurons that fire together, wire together." Hebb, D. O. 1949. *The Organization of Behavior*. N.Y.: Wiley.

[6]"A wide range of studies now confirms that development is a product of the effect of experience on genetic potential." Siegle, Daniel J. 1999. *The Developing Mind; How Relationships and the Brain Interact*. New York: Guilford Press, p.18.

[7]Begley, Sharon. 2007. *Train Your Mind; Change Your Brain; How a New Science Reveals our Extraordinary Ability to Change Ourselves*. New York: Ballentine Books.

[8]"Intersubjectivity gives meaning to interactions." Stern, D.N. 1985. *The Interpersonal World of the Infant*. New York: Basic Books, p.136.

[9]Perry, Glenn. 1998. *Essays on Psychological Astrology*. San Raphael, California: AAP. Greene & Sasportas. 1992. *The Luminaries; The Psychology of the Sun and Moon in the Horoscope*. York Beach: Samuel Weiser, Inc.

[10]"A sign can describe a multi-generational transmission process." Bowen, M., Kerr, M.E. 1988. *Family Evaluation*. N.Y.: W.W.Norton & Co., Inc., pp. 221-255.

[11]Star, Gloria. 2000. *Astrology & Your Child: A Handbook for Parents*. St. Paul: Llewellyn Publications, p. 250.

[12]Greene, Brian R. 1999. *The Elegant Universe; Superstrings, Hidden Dimensions, and the Quest for the Ultimate Theory*. New York: W. W. Norton & Company, Ltd., pp. 120-121.

[13]Sedgwick, Phillip. 1989. *The Sun at the Center*. St. Paul: Llewellyn Publications.

[14]"Ingber introduced the concept of tensegrity to capture the way the structural wholeness of a cell is maintained when it is exposed to pressures of a changing dynamic of forces." Sander, Louis W., M.D. 2002. *Thinking Differently; Principles of Process in Living Systems and the Specificity of Being Known* from Psychoanalytic Dialogues, 12(1):11-42. Boston: The Analytic Press, p. 17.

[15]Greene, Liz & Sasportas, Howard. 1992. *The Luminaries; The Psychology of the Sun and Moon in the Horoscope*. York Beach: Samuel Weiser, Inc., p. 9.

Chapter Four

[1]Bowlby, J. 1969. *Attachment and Loss*; Vol. 1. New York: Basic Books.

[2]Stern, Daniel N. 1985. *The Interpersonal World of the Infant*. N.Y.: Basic Books.

[3]Siegle, Daniel J. 1999. *The Developing Mind; How Relationships and the Brain Interact*. New York: Guilford Press.

[4]Fraley, R. Chris. 2004. *A Brief Overview of Adult Attachment Theory and Research*. www.psych.uiuc.edu/~refraley/attachment.htm.

[5]Stern, Daniel N. 1985. *The Interpersonal World of the Infant*. N.Y.: Basic Books, pp. 26-34.

[6]Siegle, Daniel J. 1999. *The Developing Mind; How Relationships and the Brain Interact*. New York: Guilford Press, p. 307.

[7]Sheldrake, Rupert. 1989. *The Presence of the Past; Morphic Resonance and the Habits of Nature.* New York: Vintage Books.

[8]Grinspoon, David. 2003. *Lonely Planets; The Natural Philosophy of Alien Life.* New York: HarperCollins Publishers, Inc.

[9]Whitmont, E.C. 1969. *The Symbolic Quest.* Princeton, NJ: University Press.

Chapter Five

[1]"Windows of development." Schore, Allan. 1994. *Affect Regulation and the Origin of the Self; The Neurobiology of Emotional Development.* Hillsdale, NJ. Earlbaum, p. 11. *Emotional Development.* Hillsdale, NJ. Earlbaum. and Crain, William. 2000. *Theories of Development; Concepts and Applications.* N.Y: Prentice Hall, p. 66.

[2]"Continuous versus discontinuous development." Crain, William. 2000. *Theories of Development; Concepts and Applications*. N.Y: Prentice Hall, pp. 287-290.

[3]Schore, Allan. 1994. *Affect Regulation and the Origin of the Self; The Neurobiology of Emotional Development.* Hillsdale, NJ. Earlbaum.

[4]Srouffe, L.A. 1996. *Emotional Development: The organization of emotional life in the early years.* New York: Cambridge University Press.

[5]"By the eighth month of the first year of life, the attachment relationship between child and mother is formed." Crain, William. 2000. *Theories of Development; Concepts and Applications* N.Y: Prentice Hall, p. 49.

[6]"The emergent self." Stern, Daniel N. 1985. *The Interpersonal World of the Infant.* N.Y.: Basic Books, pp. 37-68.

[6]Srouffe, L.A. 1996. *Emotional Development: The organization of emotional life in the early years.* New York: Cambridge University Press.

[7]"The core self, the emergent self." Stern, Daniel N. 1985. *The Interpersonal World of the Infant.* N.Y.: Basic Books, pp. 69-123.

[8]"The verbal self." Ibid., pp. 162-182.

[9]"One function is the ability for the child to narrate his own story based upon a sense of continuity over time." This is called autonoesis. Siegle, Daniel J. 1999. The Developing Mind; How Relationships and the Brain Interact, New York: Guilford Press.p.35

[10]Stern, Daniel N. 1985. *The Interpersonal World of the Infant.* N.Y.: Basic Books, p. 10.

[11]Panksepp, Jaak. 1998. *Affective Neuroscience; The Foundations of Human and Animal Emotions.* N.Y.: Oxford Press.

[12]"Genogram." Bowen, M., Kerr, M.E. 1988. *Family Evaluation.* N.Y.: W.W. Norton & Co., Inc.

[13]Srouffe, L.A. 1996. *Emotional Development: The organization of emotional life in the early years.* New York: Cambridge University Press.

[14] Davies, Douglas (1999) *Child Development* N.Y: Guilford Press.

[15] "Mahler." Crain, William. 2000. *Theories of Development; Concepts and Applications.* N.Y: Prentice Hall.pp.299-314.

Chapter Six

[1] Srouffe, L.A. 1996. *Emotional Development: The organization of emotional life in the early years.* New York: Cambridge University Press.

[2] Ibid.

[3] Ibid.

[4] Davies, Douglas. 1999. *Child Development.* N.Y: Guilford Press.

[5] Srouffe, L.A. 1996. *Emotional Development: The organization of emotional life in the early years.* New York: Cambridge University Press.

[6] Ibid.

[7] "There is a Moon-Moon opposition during this time." Costello, Darby. 1996. *The Astrological Moon.* London: CPA Press, pp. 166-172.

[8] Srouffe, L.A. 1996. Emotional Development: The organization of emotional life in the early years. New York: Cambridge University Press.

[9] Ibid.

[10] Panksepp, Jaak. 1998. *Affective Neuroscience; The Foundations of Human and Animal Emotions.* N.Y.: Oxford Press, p. 9.

[11] Sheehy, Gail. 1976. *Passages; Predictable Crises of Adult Life.* N.Y.: E. P. Dutton.

[12] Ibid.

[13] Panksepp, Jaak. 1998. *Affective Neuroscience; The Foundations of Human and Animal Emotions.* N.Y.: Oxford Press.

[14] Sheehy, Gail. 1976. *Passages; Predictable Crises of Adult Life.* N.Y.: E. P. Dutton.

[15] Ibid.

Chapter Seven

[1] Stern, Daniel N. 1985. *The Interpersonal World of the Infant.* N.Y.: Basic Books. pp. 27-33.

[2] Schore, Allan. 1994. *Affect Regulation and the Origin of the Self; The Neurobiology of Emotional Development.* Hillsdale, NJ. Earlbaum. p.7.

[3] Miller, Alan S., Kanazawa, S. 2007. *Why Beautiful People have More Daughters.* N.Y.: Penguin Group.

[4] Panksepp, Jaak. 1998. *Affective Neuroscience; The Foundations of Human and Animal Emotions.* N.Y.: Oxford Press, p. 290.

[5] Schore, Allan. 1994. *Affect Regulation and the Origin of the Self; The Neurobiology of Emotional Development.* Hillsdale, NJ: Earlbaum.

[6] "The Lunar Return Theory of development is also multi-layered; twelve aspects of self can evolve simultaneously once they have all emerged." Multi-linear development also described in developmental psychology by Crain, William. 2000. *Theories of Development; Concepts and Applications* N.Y: Prentice Hall and by Stern, Daniel N. 1985. *The Interpersonal World of the Infant.* N.Y.: Basic Books.p. 20-23.

Chapter Eight

[1] "Chaos theory." Gleick, James. 1987. *Chaos: Making A New Science.* New York: Viking Penguin, Inc.

[2] Brady, Bernadette. 1999. *Predictive Astrology, The Eagle and the Lark.* York Beach: Samuel Weiser.

[3] Clark, Brian. 1999. *The Progressed Moon; Mnemosyne's Recollections.* Issue 4, December 1999 *Appolon.* London: CPA.

Chapter Nine

[1] Clark, Brian. 1999. *The Progressed Moon; Mnemosyne's Recollections.* Issue 4, December 1999. *Appolon.* London: CPA, p. 29.

[2] Siegle, Daniel J. 1999. *The Developing Mind; How Relationships and the Brain Interact.* New York: Guilford Press.

[3] "Self object function." Wolfe, Ernest, S. 1988. *Treating the Self; Elements of Clinica Self-Psychology.* N.Y.: Guilford Press, p 26.

[4] Sheldrake, Rupert. 1989. *The Presence of the Past; Morphic Resonance and the Habits of Nature.* New York: Vintage Books.

Chapter Ten

[1] Clark, Brian. 1999. *The Progressed Moon; Mnemosyne's Recollections.* Issue 4, December 1999. *Appolon.* London: CPA.

[2] Costello, Darby. 1996. *The Astrological Moon.* London: CPA Press. p. 153.

[3] Star, Gloria. 2000. *Astrology & Your Child: A Handbook for Parents.* St. Paul: Llewellyn Publications, p. 269.

[4] Arroyo, Stephen. 1978. *Astrology, Karma, & Transformation; The Inner Dimensions of the Birth Chart.* Sebastopol, California: CRCS Publications, pp.176-182.

[5] "The lunation cycle." Rudyar, Dane. 1978. *The Practice of Astrology.* Boulder, Colorado: Shambhala.

[6]Costello, Darby. 1996. *The Astrological Moon*. London: CPA Press.

[6]Merriman, Ray. 1991. *Evolutionary Astrology: The Journey of the Soul Through the Horoscope.* Seek-It Publications.

[7]Tronick, E.Z., Als, H. Adamson, L., Wise, S., & Brazelton, T. 1978. "The Infant's Response to Entrapment between Contradictory Messages in Face-to-Face Interactions." *American Child Psychiatry*, pp. 17:1-13.

[8]"Evolutionary psychology stakes its claim on the genetic inscriptions of evolution and the subcortical (animal) brain." Panksepp, Jaak. 1998. *Affective Neuroscience; The Foundations of Human and Animal Emotions*. N.Y.: Oxford Press, p.123.

[9]Ibid.

[10]Iyengar, B. K. S. 1966. *Light on Yoga*. New York: Schoken Books, Inc., pp. 17-19.

References

American Academy of Child and Adolescent Psychiatry. 1997. *Normal Adolescent Development.* www.aacap.org/publications/factsfam/develop.htm

Arroyo, Stephen. 1978. *Astrology, Karma, & Transformation; The Inner Dimensions of the Birth Chart.* Sebastopol, California: CRCS Publications.

Begley, Sharon. .2007. Train Your Mind, Change Your Brain; How a New Science Reveals Our Extraordinary Ability to Change Ourselves. New York: Ballentine.

Brady, Bernadette. 1999. *Predictive Astrology, The Eagle and the Lark.* York Beach: Samuel Weiser.

Bowen, M., Kerr, M.E. 1988. *Family Evaluation*, N.Y.: W.W. Norton & Co., Inc.

Bowers, Michael and Gautney, Karen. 2006. *Family Therapy Magazine*, Alexandria, VA: AAMFT, September-October.

Bowlby, J. 1969. *Attachment and Loss*; Vol. 1. New York: Basic Books.

Bowlby, J. 1973. *Attachment and Loss*: Vol. 2. New York: Basic Books.

Bowlby, J. 1980. *Attachment and Loss*: Vol. 3. New York: Basic Books.

Clark, Brian. 1999. *The Progressed Moon; Mnemosyne's Recollections*. Issue 4, December 1999. *Appolon.* London: CPA.

Clark, Brian. 1999. *The Progressed Moon.* www.AstroSynthesis.com.au.

Crain, William. 2000. *Theories of Development; Concepts and Applications* N.Y: Prentice Hall.

Costello, Darby. 1996. *The Astrological Moon*. London: CPA Press.

Damasio, A.R. 1994. *Descartes' Error; Emotion, reason and the human brain*. New York: Grosset/Putnam.

Davies, Douglas. 1999. *Child Development* . N.Y: Guilford Press.

Deak, Joanna, Ph.d. 2002. *Girls will be Girls; Raising Confident and Courageous Daughters*. N.Y.: Hyperion Books.

Fraley, R. Chris. 2004. *A Brief Overview* of *Adult Attachment Theory and Research*. www.psych.uiuc.edu/~refraley/attachment.htm

Frost, R. 1946. *The Complete Poems of Robert Frost*. New York: Modern Library.

Greene, Brian R. 1999. *The Elegant Universe; Superstrings, Hidden Dimensions, and the Quest for the Ultimate Theory*. New York: W. W. Norton & Company, Ltd.

Greene, Liz & Sasportas, Howard. 1992. *The Luminaries; The Psychology of the Sun and Moon in the Horoscope*. York Beach: Samuel Weiser, Inc.

Grinspoon, David. 2003. *Lonely Planets; The Natural Philosophy of Alien Life*, New York: HarperCollins Publishers, Inc.

Gleick, James. 1987. *Chaos: Making A New Science*. New York: Viking Penguin, Inc.

Harness, Dennis. 2000. *Hindu Dasha System–Exploring Predictive Planetary Periods*. Anaheim, ISAR Conference 2000: Tape ISR20-054, Sun Recording Service.

Huber, Bruno. 1996. *Astrological Psychosynthesis*. York Beach: Samuel Weiser, Inc.

Hyde, Maggie. 1992. *Jung and Astrology*. Northampton, England: Aquarian Press.

Lawton, Glennys. 2003. *Attachment Styles and Adult Relationships*. Anaheim, ISAR Conference 2003: Tape ISR23-041, Sun Recording Service.

Merriman, Ray. 1991. *Evolutionary Astrology: The Journey of the Soul Through the Horoscope*. Seek-It Publications.

Miller, Alan S., Kanazawa, S. 2007. *Why Beautiful People have More Daughters*. N.Y.: Penguin Group.

Moskowitz, M., Monk, C., Kaye, C., Ellman, S., eds. 1997. *The Neurobiological Basis for Psychotherapeutic Intervention*. New Jersey: Jason Aronson, Ltd.

National Institute of Mental Health. 2005. *The Teen Brain: A Work in Progress*. www.familiesonlinemagazine.com

Panksepp, Jaak. 1998. *Affective Neuroscience; The Foundations of Human and Animal Emotions* N.Y.: Oxford Press.

Perry, Glenn. *Twelve Steps to Enlightenment* (available on tape), San Raphael: Association of AstroPsychology.

Pruitt, David B., ed., American Academy of Child and Adolescent Psychiatry. 1999. *Your Adolescent; Emotional, Behavioral, and Cognitive Development from Early Adolescence through the Teen Years*. N.Y.: HarperCollins Publishers.

Rudyar, Dane. 1978. *The Practice of Astrology*. Boulder, Colorado: Shambhala.

Rudhyar, Dane. 1976. *Person Centered Astrology*. New York: Aurora Press.

Ruperti, Alexander. 2005. *Cycles of Becoming*. Santa Monica: Earthwalk School of Astrology

Schore, Allan. 1994. *Affect Regulation and the Origin of the Self; The Neurobiology of Emotional Development.* Hillsdale, N.J.: Earlbaum.

Schwartz, Jeffery M. and Begley, Sharon. 2002. *The Mind & The Brain: Neuroplasticity and the Power of Mental Force.* New York: Regan Books.

Sedgwick, Phillip. 1989. *The Sun at the Center* St. Paul: Llewellyn Publications.

Sheehy, Gail (1976) *Passages; Predictable Crises of Adult Life,* N.Y.: E. P. Dutton.

Siegle, Daniel J. 1999. *The Developing Mind; How Relationships and the Brain Interact.* New York: Guilford Press.

Sheldrake, Rupert. 1989. *The Presence of the Past; Morphic Resonance and the Habits of Nature.* New York: Vintage Books.

Star, Gloria. 2000. *Astrology & Your Child: A Handbook for Parents.* St. Paul: Llewellyn Publications.

Stern, Daniel N. 1985. *The Interpersonal World of the Infant.* N.Y.: Basic Books.

Strouffe, L.A. 1996. *Emotional Development: The organization of emotional life in the early years.* New York: Cambridge University Press.

Siegle, Daniel J. 1999. *The Developing Mind; How Relationships and the Brain Interact.* New York: Guilford Press.

Stern, D.N. 1985. *The Interpersonal World of the Infant.* New York: Basic Books.

Whitmont, E.C. 1969. *The Symbolic Quest.* Princeton, NJ: University Press.

Wolfe, Ernest, S. 1988. *Treating the Self; Elements of Clinical Self-Psychology*, N.Y.: Guilford Press.

www.ingramcontent.com/pod-product-compliance
Lightning Source LLC
Chambersburg PA
CBHW080550170426
43195CB00016B/2744